A wonderfully funny, warm and engaging insight
rollercoaster ride that is parentin
will remind you that mess
the mag
Rachel Vine (Former BBC
Coach, N

Jess injects her personality ___ . elegant
writing and ability to th___ __rmly amuse makes
compelling reading and keeps you thoroughly absorbed.
Lesley Kennedy-Jones (Mum of one)

"Moments in Mummydom" serves as a reminder that the
idiosyncrasies of our relatives and the craziness of a life
lived together can be the exact things that bring us joy.
Siân Wyn Rees (Friend)

A light-hearted and warm account of funny family life
moments. There are so many relatable experiences; I
could see myself on every other page.
A must read for any Mum!
Karen Stevens (Mum of two)

I've been reading snippets of what has become this book
for years, giggling and agreeing with what's said. Jess
has, on paper, managed to communicate motherhood,
the hood once you are in, you aren't ever escaping.
Kaz Gratton (Author, Pastor, Mum of two)

MOMENTS IN MUMMYDOM

One Mummy, five kids on a
helter-skelter ride that is family life!

Dedicated to

Mum

Contents

Acknowledgements

Thanks to Rachel Patterson for first planting the idea and encouraging me to get my meandering musings into a book.

Thanks to Matt Bird, Kaz Gratton and all my fellow authors on the PublishU "Write my Book" course for doing this journey with me.

Thanks to Chris Alexander, Kaz Gratton, Emily Stanford Rowlands, Siân Wyn Rees, Karen Stevens and Rachel Vine for taking time to read early drafts and offer valuable feedback as well as support and encouragement. Massive thanks to Janet Leacock for helping me painstakingly go through and do a final edit.

Thanks to my dear husband for his support and advice during the time I spent writing, putting up with lots of late nights sat alone (although admittedly he was allowed to take his pick of whatever he wanted on the telly during this time) and generally just keeping me sane with belly laughs.

A massive thanks to all my kids, big and little, for being the treasures that you are, for giving me so much fun and urging me to go on when I've read you snippets and you've wanted to hear more. I am proud of you all and I love you more than you will ever know.

And lastly, thank you to you, my readers, for taking the time to read my book and listen to this story (which is fictional but based very heavily on fact!)

Foreword

I first met/watched Jess as she wrangled her four children into swimming lessons at a local pool – I was new to the area feeling lonely and taking on a massive work challenge.

She only ever said hi but always seemed to have it sorted. My kids didn't last long at the swimming lessons partly because the pool was the same temperature as the sea in winter and partly because they hated it and I decided I didn't want to argue all the way there and back every week.

Time moved on and that work challenge was leading a local church. I ended up preaching at her church, rather like the one which you will read of. We connected, added each other as Facebook friends.

One summer there was a writing challenge on Facebook – we met up at a pub and chatted about one day writing a book although I think hers was, at that point, much more likely.

Move forward a few years and one more baby for her and I know this ... if I'm having a day where I feel busy, I remember that in North Wales, Jess is probably arguing for the underdog in a work capacity, she will be planning to bake (she seems to find time, I've no idea how), there's always a child's birthday to plan and she's still saying yes to the waifs and strays. I look at Jess and think, it's OK, if she's got this, I've got this and that's all I need.

Kaz Gratton (Author, Pastor, Friend, Mum of two)

A wonderfully funny, warm and engaging insight into the rollercoaster ride that is parenting.

Jess's honest portrayal of life herding five children, a dog, a job and a golf-loving, undertaker husband, will make every mum feel seen, understood and – quite frankly – deserving of a medal.

If you've ever felt so sleep-deprived you can barely stand, wild with frustration at your never-ending parental to-do list and guilty at losing your cool yet again, this heartfelt diary will remind you that messy, imperfect family life is where the magic happens. Forget Instagram. You are enough.

Rachel Vine (Former BBC presenter, Women's Career Coach, Mum of two)

Before You Begin...

Hello dear Reader,

Firstly, thank you so much for taking time to read this, presumably something struck a chord as you picked it up and read the cover so let me explain,

I first started writing bits and pieces for this book as I put moments of my day on social media. I was a new parent and at that stage, I was trying to navigate looking after two small people (a newborn who did not sleep at all for the first year) and a 19-month-old. As well as exhilarating, it was a lonely place at times; amidst the sheer tiredness and being bombarded by advice from people, books, healthcare professionals... trying to work out who to listen to or whether to trust my own judgement, riding the pendulum of melting moments, when my little ones did something that just grabbed my heart and extreme self-doubt. So, I just started to put stuff out there as a kind of "is there anyone else who is having a day like this?" It turns out that quite a few people did, so there began my blog.

When I wrote this book, I thought seriously about giving this Mummy a name, but decided that keeping her as "Mummy" may mean she is more relatable as we can all put ourselves in her shoes. Also, I don't know about you, but as soon as I had kids, I became known as Mum/ Mummy/Mam by my kids and their friends. In my phone, the Mums of my kids' friends are always put in as "So and So's Mum".

As an artist, someone once told me "Comparison is the thief of creativity". I would add, comparison is the thief of joy in the moments that you are currently in. We are bombarded on a daily basis by everybody's perfect. Let's be real and make the most of the moments that we are in, the good, the bad and the really grotty. Our moments!

Love

Jess x

Prologue

December 31st, 2021

9am

"Who was that?" I looked up from the table where I was sitting having a lazy breakfast. The doorbell had just gone setting George, the dog, off on his barking frenzy. "Oh, just the post," Liam said, handing me a parcel.

"Oh!" I inspected it to see if there were any clues as to who it was from. "It's a late Christmas present." Liam sounded sheepish. "My 'leave-it-until-the-week-before Christmas' strategy didn't quite work, I was hoping it'd get here earlier, when I pressed 'Buy now'. I hadn't realised the delivery date was after Christmas and not the next day."

"Oh, thank you. What is it?" I was impressed that he left it until Christmas week and not Christmas Eve!

"Go on, open it," said Liam, he was looking rather pleased with himself. I unwrapped the packaging and there was a beautiful leather-bound journal of blank empty pages.

"Oh wow, it's gorgeous, thank you!" I looked at my husband, sometimes he did get it right with the presents. "Well, I know you've been writing bits about this past year all over the place, so I thought you might want to put it all together, so you don't lose them... a bit of a record for the kids when they are older," he says.

I was surprised he had even noticed my writing, most of it had been done in the middle of the night, on my phone, whilst feeding Isla. She is our fifth child, born this year. We seem to breed children who don't sleep during the night until they are passed the age of one.

It has been exhausting, but at the same time, with her being our fifth, I've realised that in the grand scheme of things, this bit of knackered-ness is over in the blink of an eye, so decided to embrace it (in a tired Mummy kind of way). Unlike previous night-time feeds with my other four, when I had mainly scrolled through my newsfeed on my phone, this time I thought I'd write snippets about the days from a tired Mummy's perspective. Actually, Liam's idea about putting it all in one physical place isn't a bad idea, otherwise it's destined to end up like all the photos of the kids... somewhere on a digital cloud and nothing physical to show for it (apart from Mummy-guilt). Poor Olly only got his baby book when he turned three and I found out I was expecting Isla and that I wasn't perimenopausal. The others; Nell, Maisie and Riley have got their first-year baby books and that's it, they probably won't get another photobook until they've grown up and left home at this rate.

I pull myself back to the present and look at Liam. "Do you know what? That is such a thoughtful gift, love," I say. "Thank you" as I lean over and kiss him on the cheek. Liam's suspended anticipation of my reaction shows as relief on his face.

8pm

And relax.

Kids all in bed, rubbish telly, Liam's watching some war-film... on New Year's Eve! Are we officially middle-aged? I think back to swanky parties and games nights, Murder Mysteries and fireworks... now I can't even manage staying up to watch the fireworks on the telly, I even got Liam to record it last year and I watched it with the kids in the morning... how rock and roll am I?!

Sitting here with a New Year's Eve celebratory glass of Bailey's (pretty sure one glass won't affect breastfeeding?) and as is now my custom on New Year's Eve, having a think about this past year.

Let's see... pretty much... moments... not really a diary, more moments! "Moments in Mummydom".

Chapter 1
January

Retrospectively, taking four children under the age of ten to the bank for an appointment was probably not the best idea she'd ever had, despite assurances of the bank lady that "it would be fine". Such was the importance of this meeting, Mummy ignored the gnawing feeling that perhaps this may not go to plan and undeterred, pressed on, actually arriving on time for her appointment which was no small feat with her crew to organise; Nell, the eldest, was nine; Maisie was seven, Riley was five and Olly was three.

This meeting was important because just over a month ago, Mummy had been feeling a bit not herself, so she had snuck a cheap pregnancy test into the basket during her supermarket shop, hidden under the cheese until she got to the self-checkout. This was mainly to rule out pregnancy and to embrace the next phase of her life being peri-menopausal; brain-fog, tiredness, intermittent periods and a daily hormonal rollercoaster. She was showing all the symptoms.

It was much to her surprise, then, that two blue lines appeared before her very eyes and confirmed that she was indeed pregnant. Understandably, she was feeling a little overawed by this and had waited a good twenty-four hours to break the news to Daddy whilst she tried to get her head round the fact that in medical terms, she had already been classed as a "geriatric" mother at the ripe old age of thirty-five, so what would this make her now she was forty-four? Daddy's immediate thought upon being told the news was, "well, at least we don't need to change the car". Mummy then pointed out that although the car was large enough, the house wasn't and would need extending, or they'd have to move. So, this was the day of persuading the bank to lend them the money for an extension.

Having swept through the bank foyer like a hurricane, retrieving various children from doing 'twizzies' on the revolving chairs, Mummy had used the alone-time in the lift to reiterate the stern warning she had already issued her offspring on their way into town.

What Mummy hadn't factored in was that sons, Riley and Olly, had spent half of the night in a tag team effort to keep Mummy awake and sneak into her bed. Cooperative sons were therefore in short supply and Nice Mummy hadn't yet made an appearance as Knackered Mummy had taken over. Somehow Daddy always managed to sleep through any tag team efforts to get into parental bed and could happily snore his way through the two heat-seeking missiles lying, squirming and pushing, in the middle of the bed.

Nice Bank Lady, a Miss (so no children yet, she told Mummy), remained professional as she ushered Mummy and her troop into the office. The children sat nicely and Mummy felt smug.

"So, we'll be needing to take into account the rising rates of inflation, I'm afraid," the bank lady explained as youngest son, Olly, squirmed and struggled in Mummy's lap until she let him loose.

"I see," said Mummy, not entirely sure what was being said because now Olly was trying to push Riley off his chair with an ensuing tussle. "Do you mind if I just..." said Mummy, giving both boys her best Mum-look and issuing a muttered threat out of the corner of her mouth as her two sons were failing to pipe-down.

At this point, Riley, having lost his chair to a triumphant three-year old, had decided to focus on making carpet angels. He lay on his back, arms and legs moving like windscreen wipers and asked loudly if he'd made a carpet angel yet.

Meanwhile, Olly began to clutch himself, announcing that he needed a wee-wee and asking whether he could just go and pee outside on the street like the doggy they had seen on the way there. Mummy looked apologetically at the Bank Lady and told her youngest son to wait as he had only just been twenty minutes earlier. Olly was increasingly insistent and Mummy explained there was no toilet there for him to use. Nice Bank Lady, realising not much was going to get done until this bladder matter was addressed, eventually offered to go and check with the Bank Manager whether Olly and Riley could have clearance to use the staff toilets. Clearance was given and she led the way as daughters, Nell and Maisie, continued to be on their best behaviour, sitting quietly in the office.

Mummy helped youngest with toilet as older son went into the cubicle next door. Meanwhile Bank Lady waited outside cubicles (obviously having been instructed to ensure that these two feral boys didn't turn into Butch Cassidy and the Sundance Kid once they got into the inner sanctum of the staff toilets). Mummy suddenly heard

Riley emit a rip-roaring fart from the cubicle next door and she quickly flushed the chain to hide the noise, avoiding eye contact with the Bank Lady on her way out.

Back in the office, Nice Bank Lady went through final questions about health. "Do you drink over twenty-eight units of alcohol a week?" Mummy responded: "No, although possibly after this morning's appointment I may well do!"

Released, Mummy picked up remnants of her dignity and said her thank yous and goodbyes to Nice Bank Lady.

Outside, following a full-blown rollicking from Mummy, sons reverted to Well-behaved and Cooperative after their raucous behaviour which had surely given Nice Bank Lady some food for thought with regards to future possibilities of offspring.

Having received the "Yes" from Nice Bank Lady, Mummy had already organised everyone in terms of contractors, so building work commenced a mere two weeks later. Mummy, you see, in addition to dealing with her clan, also works part-time as a manager of a number of supported housing projects. Unbeknownst to the builder, he was going to be project managed to within an inch of his life. Daddy had decided to leave his wife to it as he was busy managing his own business as a Funeral Director. He also knew better than to attempt an intervention with a hormonal, nesting Mummy in Manager mode. Mummy was anticipating some disarray in the house but was attempting to file the thought somewhere in her mind that the means would justify the end, a thought that she hoped to pull out whenever the mess got beyond what she could mentally handle.

As yet, Mummy and Daddy had kept the news of expecting number five to themselves. Mummy found out she was expecting after doing a rapid pee on a stick before running her two girls to gymnastics one morning.

For some reason with babies one to four, Mummy had always found out that she was pregnant when Daddy was on a fishing trip and Daddy arrived home to the news. After the announcement of number four, Daddy gave up fishing and took up golf.

Mummy decided to break the news of number five to him before a day's golf this time, sending him on his merry way to mull over this latest family nugget. Daddy returned from golf asking whether she had thought of any names which was Daddy's way of saying that this would be great.

Two months later, Mummy had overcome nausea and at the same time the desire to eat everything in her kitchen cupboards and the second trimester was in sight. Mummy and Daddy discussed when to break this news to Nana and the rest of the world. Mummy found it hilarious that when she and Daddy first got together, seventeen years before, Nana insisted on gifting Mummy with various random DVDs of stories about Nuns. Mummy thought this was partly because Nana knew that Mummy was a Christian and partly because Daddy had a number of children from a previous relationship. Mummy wondered whether Nana hoped that the aura of Nuns would grace their house. Five children later and Nana had well and truly left that idea behind.

Mummy had also not yet broken the news to her employer. Mummy had worked for this charity for a very long time and moved around within the organisation. Ordinarily Mummy would have got itchy feet a very long time ago, but work offered her enough variety to keep her interested. Indeed, some days were quite surreal. This particular day, for example, Mummy received a phone call from a client in distress.

"Hello?" answered Mummy.

Huge sobs over the phone and then a tumble of words from client: "Oh it's just horrible, I can't deal with it, I need someone to come over and help..." Mummy was slightly alarmed, as she realised it was Lil, one of the ladies who had recently moved in. "What's the matter Lil?" "It's Dave and Dora," Lil said. Mummy tried to delve into the depths of her brain and remember who Dave and Dora were. "Dave? Dora?" she asked, hoping that further light would be shed on the matter. Lil launched off: "They're dead... I don't know about Fred and Ginger though... I just covered the tank and left them, I couldn't face it," said Lil.

Fish... thought Mummy, relieved as Lil could at times sail very close to the wind when it came to the criminal justice system... Dave and Dora were fish!

Dave and Dora appeared to be dead following a fish-tank cleaning exercise. Half an hour later, Mummy arrived outside the house to find Lil hovering about on the street, unable to go inside because of the fish debacle as she stated the smell was making her wretch. Mummy wondered how her pregnancy-heightened sense of smell would fare. She entered the flat and there in the corner of the lounge was the tank. Sure enough, Dora and Dave were very much dead. Fred and Ginger were nowhere to be seen. Mummy extracted Dora and Dave with the fish net and carried them to the bathroom, whereupon she chucked them in the loo and flushed the chain. This is when Mummy made the discovery that dead fish don't flush, as the lifeless Dora and Dave were still bobbing around the toilet bowl post toilet flush. She couldn't very well leave them there, could she? Lil was already traumatised enough.

As Mummy found herself on her hands and knees, retrieving floating fish from the toilet bowl with a fish net, she did wonder which part of her job description covered this particular task. Plan B was to dispose of them in the bin. Fred and Ginger, it turned out, were happily swimming around in a smaller tank in the kitchen and Mummy found the leftovers of the previous night's curry in the bin, so hid Dora and Dave amidst the leftovers, hoping that the smell of curry would mask the smell of dead fish. Lil happily returned to her flat. "All in a day's work," thought Mummy.

"SOMETIMES THIS working Mummy lark is blooming hard work," thought Mummy one cold Wednesday a week later as she sat in the warmth of the Spectator gallery at the Leisure Centre, watching Olly and Riley swim. It had been a day and a half!

It had started with her asking Riley and Olly to get dressed a zillion times, discovering that her requests had gone unheeded and Riley was still in his pyjamas at 8:20am, ten minutes after breakfast should have been consumed and ten minutes before they were due to leave. Mummy was in full rant mode on the way to school/ nursery and sons had been told they could not descend on a school morning without being fully dressed and screens of any description were absolutely banned forever more on school days.

Work was work; full-on with a plethora of different people, different problems, different quirks, "colourful characters" etc. It got to 2pm and Mummy realised lunch was not going to happen before work finished.

School pick-up was as usual, with Mummy, the mad woman, hot-tailing it through the school gates, late.

They'd had a quick turnaround at home, at which point Mummy shoved a slice of toast down to stave off queasiness and then ferried everyone to the car ready for the after-school activities. In her wisdom, Mummy had crammed as many activities as she could all into one evening to try and kid herself that she actually had a life beyond taxiing everyone around. She had begun to question her decision as they arrived at the pool. Olly, already in his swimming costume and goggles, raring to go, was deposited with the teacher in the pool and Mummy went to put his shoes in his bag... BAG... WHERE WAS THE BAG?? Mummy ran back to the car. No bag. She scoured the changing room. No bag. Bag was at home along with towel and clothes.

She had hastily asked swimming-parent friend to watch her offspring and high-tailed it back home to find the bag, which was on the kitchen floor being chewed by the aged hound.

When Mummy arrived back at the pool, having extracted Olly from the pool, replacing him with Riley, she'd collapsed in the spectators' gallery together with a much-needed Cost-a-Fortune coffee and a mashed and mullered excuse for a brain as her youngest did the floss with his pals.

MUMMY WAS having a stand-up-on-the-go-lunch at her kitchen counter, reminding herself that she needed to eat amidst the day that was officially her "day off". Her "day off" was actually her busiest day where she didn't sit down but attempted to do all the household chores in one day and clocked up a grand sixteen kilometres just walking around her house, her new watch told her. The phone rang.

School. Immediately Mummy wondered which child was ill.

"Nothing to worry about," said School Miss, kindly, "We are just ringing as we have noticed that Riley has been late to school ten times since September."

"Just out of interest," asked Mummy, "how is it that just one of them is late when I have dropped four of them off at the same school door at the same time each morning?"

Miss ignored this. "We are just wondering whether there is anything that we can do to help so that you can get your child to school on time?"

Mummy thought, yes, as a matter of fact, come round and get up at the crack of dawn, sort out all the lunches and the evening meal, feed the dog and the cat, yell at the dog (quietly) as she is barking outside and it is only six o'clock, then remind two of my offspring at least three times whilst they are downstairs that they need to go upstairs and get dressed, only to find them still in pyjamas ten minutes later after you have come out of the shower, so remind them again twice, give up and dress them yourself. Then give offspring breakfast (after asking them five times to come to the table and then after three times of trying to find out what they want for breakfast), only to have 'threenager' change his mind after you have got him what he has requested, then wash up whilst kicking the dog outside again for a wee and ordering children to clean their teeth, then go upstairs to clean your own teeth and find both sons nowhere near the bathroom, in their room, emptying contents of dressing up box out to onto floor already covered in Lego as Olly looks for a superman figure he doesn't possess (and never has possessed) and you look for his missing shoe which has mysteriously disappeared in the five minutes since you sent him upstairs (despite it having been on his foot on his way up)... clean teeth of said offspring, leg it downstairs grabbing forgotten lunchbags on the way to the car only to have Olly say he needs the loo (quick return to house to get him to loo before there's an accident), finally get into car and drive past two schools and a college, stuck behind slow vehicles, whilst Riley counts down how many minutes late you are and you self-talk and tell yourself you are bloody brilliant and not to worry about being late, given the obstacles your offspring have thrown at you in the two hours since they woke up...

"Is there anything we can do to help?" Miss repeated as Mummy went silent whilst she settled her hormonal self.

"Nope," said Mummy, "I am aware we do arrive a couple of minutes late sometimes, but that is not due to lack of effort on my part, believe you me... I am on it..."

"Would you like to drop them at breakfast club?" offered Miss.

"No, I like to have a family breakfast," (and that would just entail the same amount of effort but starting an hour earlier, so actually no point me even going to bed if you look at it that way, plus Mummy thought that because she then sometimes goes on to complete a nine-hour day in paid work, breakfast might be the only meal she got to have with her kids).

Miss admitted some children came to school not having had any breakfast at all.

Mummy assured Miss that she would do her utmost to run the gauntlet of the school run earlier...

Miss was suitably pacified and phone call ended.

Mummy sat down and started to eat her now cold lunch with a dollop of tears on top as she just felt tired, hormonal. She had needed that phone call like a hole in the head. She knew it wasn't the intention of the school, but she took it like a slight on her parenting, when she was juggling a million balls and really trying her hardest, the slightest bit of criticism deflated her. She told herself she was doing a good job and that in the grand scheme of things arriving at 9am instead of 8:55am ten times out of a total of ninety wasn't the end of the world if it meant that she had successfully managed to clothe and feed and chat with and listen to her children prior to them beginning their school day.

"Quite frankly," she said to herself, "that we even manage to get to school at all is a minor miracle some days."

THE FOLLOWING day it had snowed... a lot... so to Mummy's relief, the school run was avoided completely as school was shut. Unlike other countries, who shrug and don the winter tyres, the whole of the United Kingdom comes to a complete standstill the minute there is a millimetre of snow.

Mummy and her clan dug out the plastic sleds from the shed, avoiding the gaping hole that had been dug in the back garden ready for the footings for the extension. They carefully drove to the nearest place where there was a hill and a smattering of snow. Most of the morning was fun, but with intermittent arguing over whose turn it was to use the sledge. Mummy's suggestion to also use a black bag doubled over to slide on was met with "harrumphs" by her children. As the morning trawled on towards lunch, with more and more people arriving, snow melting and the ever increasing risk of one of her children (whose sled-steering skills were in desperate need of refinement) ploughing through the other small children, sending them flying like skittles, Mummy managed to coax everyone back to the car. They were just about to start home when Nana rang and asked whether Mummy wanted some help as she offered to take the children for the afternoon. Mummy agreed to this suggestion rather more quickly than she should have. "Thank you, Nana, you are a star."

Mummy felt that her very bones were tired. That afternoon, in a moment of quiet, catching up with herself, Mummy observed her growing belly and wondered what her little one would be like; who he or she would be. She wondered whether this little one already dreamt and what they thought about as they were being knitted together. She marvelled when she thought that the only One who knew was the Craftsman knitting this little one together. This little one, not yet known by the world, was completely known by Him. "And once we arrive," she reflected, "our journey is to discover the fullness we can have by coming to the realisation that we are completely known, completely sought after and completely loved by Him. He loves our very bones. He loves my tired bones," she reminded herself," we've got this..."

After a completely relaxed afternoon, Mummy collected her kids from Nana's. They'd arrived home with Olly asking for a gym jumper and Maisie asking for Ivy Propen. Although Mummy had a linguistic background, she was left stumped. Daddy arrived home just as Mummy was trying to divert a major kick-off from Olly who was still going on about a gym jumper. Mummy finally deduced that he wanted his temperature taken. Nana had commented he had red cheeks. Nana thought she was a bit of an aficionado on illnesses. Red cheeks had nothing to do with illness and everything to do with Nana whacking the heating on to sauna levels the minute there was a cloud in the sky. Snow would necessitate even hotter than usual levels. Ivy Propen, it turned out, was not a new house guest or school friend, but actually Ibuprofen. Maisie had a headache (probably also due to the tropical climate at Nana's).

Chapter 2

February

News of Mummy and Daddy's impending arrival had now broken and children were extremely excited. Nana (Daddy's Mum) needed some convincing. Opa (Mummy's Dad) was delighted. Both Daddy and Mummy had lost Grandad (Daddy's Dad) and Oma (Mummy's Mum) in the same year. It had been a tough few years. School runs had been accompanied by discussions about how the baby had got into Mummy's tummy and whether baby would be a boy or a girl. Mummy had opted for the biological explanation but had missed out a few key ingredients with an "ask Daddy when you get home".

Back garden was by the day becoming less of an excavation site. Victorian rubbish had been unearthed, namely Victorian murder bottles (which sounded horrific, much to the kids' delight), alongside rubble, roof-tiles, wood and a whole lot of rammel which aged hound insisted on bringing into the house. One previously white and ginger Tom cat was now a mucky ginger colour as he had discovered that he could slide down the side of the trench into a whole new underground playground beneath the house and then emerge and climb all over the house, leaving a trail of paw prints behind him. The level of dirt in the house was significantly more as access to the house was through the building site and children could not resist jumping on mounds of earth piled high on their way in (and out for that matter). Kids were increasingly looking like street urchins when they were dropped off at school.

Mummy had found that her aged hound was increasingly doddery and wondered how long she was going to last.

Mummy was also feeling just a little bit smug that she had managed to get all four kids to school on time this week and, according to Nell, Miss Late Monitor (who phoned Mummy last Friday) overslept the previous day and was late to school.

MUMMY CONGRATULATED herself at finding a screwed up, yogurt-covered note in Olly's lunch-bag the previous week informing her that the nursery class were going to have a Superhero party this Wednesday. Miraculously, the day dawned and she actually remembered (although not in time to get a contributory item of party food from a mad dash to Aldi), so she flung into his bag a packet of unopened biscuits which she had hidden in her secret stash in the far corner at the back of the cupboard, so Daddy didn't get them. Thankfully, Olly decided he was too hot to go as a Superhero, saving Mummy from a meltdown in more ways than one as Batman outfit was two sizes too small, so a mutual agreement was reached that normal own-clothes was a better idea.

Mummy and Olly rocked up at nursery and Mummy told teacher that he had decided not to be a Superhero as he was too hot. Teacher looked somewhat bemused by this revelation. Mummy sneaked a peek into classroom to find Olly happily settling himself down between UNIFORM clad classmates. It was Mummy's turn to look befuddled... Mummy asked Teacher: "Is it not a Superhero party today?" Teacher had no idea what Mummy was going on about. Mummy hastily removed packet of biscuits from her son's lunch-bag and retreated to her car, hiding biscuits so it didn't look like she had a touch of the munchies already.

Only later that day, when Mummy relayed this to her other offspring as she collected them from After School Club did it all become clear. It WAS a Superhero party for a nursery class that day... in a completely different school across town. Somehow, the previous week at After School Club (which catered for various schools in the area) the party note had been put in the wrong bag.

Mummy was pleased to discover that she hadn't completely lost the plot and very thankful that she had dropped off son at school as himself rather than Batman.

EARLY MORNING wake-up call from Olly; Mummy coaxed the wriggle-monster back to his own bed with the promise of a Thomas sticker in the morning, in the vain hope he might drop off back to sleep, then found out "morning" was actually only ten minutes away much to knackered Mummy's dismay.

Dragged sorry-Mummy-body downstairs to find aged hound had yet again left a large puddle, mainly because hound couldn't be harassed to go outside at Mummy's bidding the previous night.

Mummy spent the first ten minutes of her Monday morning cleaning up dog wee with ritualistic spraying of neat vinegar on floorboards (Aldi staff were now wondering whether Mummy was actually drinking the stuff, so often did she buy it). The wee smell was neutralised and the downstairs instead smelled like a chippy.

Amazingly, Mummy made it to school on time even though that involved 15 minutes of delay tactics from Riley alongside five requests that teeth be cleaned.

A long day in work was then completed and Mummy arrived home with kids fetched from Nana's en-route, just as Horace (latest named storm) decided to unleash himself on the garden furniture. Mummy found the two metre-squared toughened glass table-top in hedge and decided to bring it inside for safe-keeping.

Horace threatened to launch Mummy off into space with her newly-acquired toughened glass flying carpet. Mummy stubbornly hung on for dear life, determined that as she had spent the afternoon waging war on the criminal underbelly of the local drug cartel, she was not about to be outdone by some poxy table-top and an eighty plus mile per hour wind (although Mummy did momentarily wonder whether she had slightly underestimated the wind speed and the fact that the table-top was actually bigger than her. She manoeuvred her way to the front door. "Open the door," she ordered Nell, slightly panicked. Having finally managed to deposit manhandled glass top in hallway, Mummy found Daddy supping a cuppa in front of the telly, oblivious to his wife's escapades outside.

Just as she was about to take her coat off, Riley, the poppet, announced that he had left his school shoes at

Nana's. Mummy headed off, muttering rather ungraciously, to do round two with Horace in her quest for the forgotten school shoes.

EVERY MORNING, Mummy attempts to make time with the kids at breakfast to read a Bible verse and have a quick discussion; something positive that everyone can take into the day with them. Varying degrees of success at these as Olly is prone to going off on a tangent. He came home from Sunday kids at church one day and told Mummy all about a bloke called John eating snails in the jungle; The Gospel according to Olly. The Gospel according to Riley had Moses arriving in the desert in a helicopter, which sounded more like the opening to a Bond film than the Old Testament.

One particular morning, after sorting out initial argument about whose turn it was to sit in Daddy's chair (Daddy didn't do breakfast unless he was paying for it in a hotel), Mummy thought it quite apt that the day's topic was peace... living in peace and having peace in our hearts. She finished off with a prayer asking for peace in their hearts and their heads. Olly piped up, "Mummy, I don't like peas, I don't want peas in my head or my heart." Mummy sent up a quick arrow prayer about needing strength or something along those lines.

DESPITE MUMMY having requested that the builders ensure that the cat was locked in the house before they laid the concrete base to the extension and builders having assured Mummy that they definitely saw the cat in the house after laying concrete base, cat had definitely disappeared. Mummy and Daddy lifted floorboards at the front of the house and spent time on their hands and knees shouting for him to no avail.

Five days later, in a rare moment of quiet on a lunch break at home, Daddy heard a meowing, followed the noise, lifted the floorboards and behold, the cat emerged, covered in cobwebs from under the floor. Cat seemed none the worse and quickly settled back in. Mummy thought he must have survived on a diet of rodents during his incarceration underground.

HALF TERM... ahh now there's a thing. Daddy was stacked out with work, so it was down to Mummy to take some leave and amuse her cherubs. Mummy had quickly discovered that the thing not to do during school holidays was make the mistake of looking at social media as she was bombarded with pictures of perfect families on days out (that when costed by Mummy, would have involved half the family monthly income being spent to fund one day). This just served to send Mummy on a Guilt-Fest, so instead, she eliminated social media from her life for a week, decided to live her life instead of looking at other people's and a balance was struck of some down-time and some activities each day.

Having spent the previous day trying to stop four children from getting too close to the mallet and pickaxe that were in full swing knocking down the external wall to join pending new kitchen with existing dining room, Mummy decided it was an idea to vacate the house and take her brood to a nearby range of hills to climb one of them along with her friend, Cara and her kids.

Upon arrival, Mummy couldn't help remembering her first visit to this hill, Moel Famau, on New Year's Day the previous year. As Mummy had never been there before, she hadn't realised that it was advisable to avoid this beauty spot on bank holidays as the World and his Wife all turned up to hike it too. Undeterred, she had arrived (eventually after a few wrong turns) and Maisie had announced that she needed the toilet. Mummy, unfamiliar with the terrain, had led her brood to what appeared to be a quiet route, off the well-trodden path, for a wild wee. In search of somewhere semi-private, they had ascended this path for a good five minutes before Mummy found somewhere suitable. Mummy instructed Maisie to "just go up there" and Maisie had climbed the bank and crouched behind a large piece of bracken, commenting that it was a bit icy. Other siblings had followed suit and Mummy thought she may as well go too.

Mummy had instructed children to "just wait there" on the path below with Olly, at this point two years old, who up until then had been sat quietly in his pushchair. Mummy ascended to bracken, avoiding other rivulets of free-running wee deposited by her offspring. As Mummy crouched down, jeans round ankles, a number of things started to happen in quick succession; Olly decided he didn't like not being able to see Mummy and let out an almighty wail whilst pointing to where Mummy was crouched (trying to not draw attention to herself). World and his Wife had decided to also veer off onto this lesser trodden path and understandably were concerned to come across four apparently unaccompanied minors, one of whom was squealing uncontrollably, but then Riley had helpfully explained that Mummy was "just up there having a wee" and at that moment Mummy had discovered that she was actually perched on ice as she started to slowly slip, in crouching position, towards concerned hikers, thus appearing like a moon over Moscow bearing her all to the well-meaning onlookers as she hurriedly attempted to reassemble her decency. Hike had been abandoned as it was icier than they had realised (nothing to do with awkwardness Mummy had felt hiking with strangers who had just had a glimpse of her bare bottom and next week's washing).

Mummy had promised herself they would walk this hill on a quieter day in the coming year. That day had arrived and mission 'Ascend Moel Famau' was accomplished without too many mishaps. Mummy also discovered that there was a public toilet a mere half a mile down the road. Mummy and Cara found an accommodating café nearby and indulged in some cake and coffee whilst their tribe of children were silenced by a mammoth hot chocolate with cream and marshmallows. Mummy was hoping for a quiet day after as they were all suitably worn-out following their substantial hike.

THE DAY after arrived and a full half-term with the kids meant that Mummy's voice had finally disappeared, so now, the kids could legitimately say that they hadn't heard her, rather than the selective deafness they often had. As Daddy was still working, Mummy had to brave the weekly supermarket shop with all four children in tow. Before entering the shop, they were under strict orders to behave and stay by the trolley. Once inside, however, all prior warnings were a long and distant memory. As Olly stepped inside the sliding doors, he caught sight of himself on the security camera and then with a "Woohoo," careered like a drunken goat through the aisles. Mummy quickly managed to catch up and lifted him into the trolley seat, despite his noisy protests. Mummy decided to try and engage Riley in finding the shopping items... amongst other things, she needed Blu Tack and cling film. Riley somehow confused the two things and before she could correct him, he was loudly saying we needed to find "a Blue Film..." leading to some smirks and slightly odd looks from fellow shoppers, who were no doubt left wondering what kind of stuff their local friendly funeral director and his wife were up to in their free time. Mummy battled on through and once back at home in her kitchen, found that most of the stuff she had bought weren't items that had been on her list, requiring a second trip which she decided to do minus children once her husband had returned home. On this second trip, Mummy may have eked it out a bit to include some extended time sitting in the car in the supermarket car park, with a milkshake, supposedly listening to the radio (she had actually dozed off and woken up twenty minutes later).

Chapter 3

March

Mummy returned to work following half term. "How was your time off?" asked one of her colleagues. Mummy had returned to work for a rest. Mummy thought back over the weekend. Friday night had been particularly broken. It had started off in the middle of the night, having found a sweating child in her bed, who had been woken up by Daddy returning from a call-out. After several kicks in the ribs/legs/stomach (take your pick) Mummy decided to transfer sleeping child back to his own bed... successfully accomplished, only to have then found that said bed was damp. So, stirring child was transferred to end of brother's bed whilst she changed the sheets. Very much awake transferred back to clean bed, except by then he had wanted to be with Mummy, so Mummy had contorted her pregnant body into small ball and lay cramped next to him until his eyes were shut. Once he was definitely asleep, Mummy quietly eased one leg over the side of his digger bed and then the rest of her body, managing to sit on Paw Patrol noisy toy in the process... child had only stirred slightly so Mummy decided best way of avoiding squeaky floorboards was to virtually commando crawl out of the room, which was easier said than done with a pregnant belly. Mission accomplished; Mummy had returned to her own bed for the remnants of the night.

Proper day had then started with the sounds of the hound pacing around downstairs, so Mummy had thought she'd sneak down and let her out. She'd fumbled her way downstairs, slipper-less and found that the aging dog had already deposited a poo in the hallway, which she had deftly stepped over, not noticing a stray dollop which she had then kicked across the floor with a right footer Ronaldo would have been proud of.

Mummy evicted the dog from the house whilst quietly whispering threats and had spent next quarter of an hour shovelling up poop and disinfecting floor and foot. Really largely the portence of the day ahead... Fast forward nine hours and Mummy had been seen carrying one kicking and screaming Threenager out of local garden centre whilst three other offspring were frog-marched behind. Rose replacement trip (last rose ended up stuck to labrador's bottom, roots and all) had been abandoned when Mummy had heard three out of four of her children screaming at each other as they had fought over one of the new garden trollies that had a car incorporated underneath it. Designed to amuse the kids, these trollies instead ensure that every garden shopping trip is as stressful as possible as kids fight over whose turn it is every time. Thankfully, day had ended with a dog walk round the lake (which was a ploy to completely tire all kids out) and Daddy doing bath time with very overtired, belligerent Threenager, whilst Mummy had walked off some stress and had returned as Nice Mummy to resume bedtime story-telling duties.

In contrast, the next day had all been going according to plan. Mummy had given up on the vain hope of any kind of sleep whilst her aged hound was still alive and had a bladder the size of a gnat (unfortunately the poo was not), so Mummy decided to embrace the early morning child-free hour and get organised. Like clockwork, hound started whimpering to go out at 5.45am, Mummy hauled her sorry body out of bed, let her out, narrowly avoiding tripping over the cat, who had somehow managed to escape eviction the previous evening and continued to fashion his claw design on bottom stair carpet.

Packed lunches done, dog fed, cat fed, cup of tea made, just about to sit down for a talk with her Maker when youngest son arrived downstairs super early, still complaining about having lost a watch that wasn't his, that was too big for him and that he couldn't yet tell the time on.

Three other children descended despite Mummy having threatened no sweetie-day / no screen-time for a week (delete as appropriate) if they descended whilst clock was any other colour than yellow. Not a blind bit of notice had been paid and clock was still very blue. Mummy not feeling quite so peaceful, sorted out drinks and headed off for a walk and some headspace, leaving Daddy as the responsible adult in the house.

Fast forward two hours... Mummy had successfully deposited all offspring at school and nursery ON TIME. Youngest was still inconsolable over the loss of the watch that wasn't his. Just as Mummy mentally checked off what she had to do that day, she remembered that a conference call was booked for later on, so went to find her phone to check what time and found out that in the madness of attempting to get out of the house promptly with all children suited and booted, she had left her phone at home.

"No problem," Mummy thought, "will just pop home and get them." House was still in semi-chaos due to ongoing building works. This day was the day of the tiler arriving (mid pre-school chaos) to put self-leveller on the floor, with strict instructions that once down it shouldn't be walked on until after 4pm.

Mummy arrived home to find tiler had indeed laid aforementioned floor. Mummy popped in through the front door, stealthily, managing to keep the feline out and away from wet self-levelling floor stuff. She grabbed her phone and went out through the front door, locked the door... For some reason she couldn't get key out of the door without leaving it unlocked. Puzzled, Mummy tried it from inside... Key was definitely not coming out. So, she decided she would lock it from the inside and leave out of the back door. "Oh, hang on, self-levelling floor still levelling... Climb out of lounge window?" she thought. "No... too pregnant... Right, self-levelling floor it is." Somehow Mummy managed to lean over, unlock the back door, open the back door, all without stepping in wet cement-like floor. She threw her handbag out of door into back yard. Next for the straddle. Mummy had overestimated her leg length slightly, also had not taken into account increased size of her pregnant belly and that gusset of tights may hinder straddle ability slightly...

So near and yet so far as Mummy's right foot defied her and landed neatly in self-levelling-not-to-be-stepped-on-until-at-least-four-o-clock-floor with all the finesse of a cat burglar after a bottle of gin.

After some self-levelling of her own (how hard can it be?), Mummy departed for the office to assume the position of responsible Services Manager with a slightly cementy boot.

Lunchtime call from one of her daughter's new teachers at school, a little concerned that Nell had been telling others, "Daddy buries people". Mummy had to give a little bit of context just to ensure that it was understood that Daddy was actually a funeral director and not a Mafia boss.

Mummy ended the day emptying out the school bags and returned packed lunches, with all fruit still intact (it would appear that her children just took the fruit out for a day trip). In addition to fruit, Mummy came across a note from the school reminding parents that it was World Book Day the following week. Mummy made a mental note not to forget. She was actually secretly impressed that school had given parents more than a day's heads up, as previous requirements for costumes had come mere hours before they were needed.

WORLD BOOK Day... That was the silver lining of Lockdown... no WBD, no Sports Days (fine if you've got a sunny day and only one child, but four rainy afternoons; a different matter) and no Christmas Fayre (where Mummy supplied the goods and then had to buy them back for double the price).

Mummy had managed to skilfully avoid taking any of her children to the supermarket in the lead-up to World Book Day, thereby avoiding any arguments and pressure to buy a costume that would only be worn once but would set Mummy's wallet back significantly. Mummy had also given strict instructions to Nana not to buy any costumes.

Imagine Mummy's delight when her two girls both fit in hand-me down costumes from the exorbitant ones that Nana had gifted the previous year and both of her boys bypassed her suggestions of going as Mikka the Mouse (which would have involved Mummy making a dubious looking mouse head out of a recycled cereal box, because her youngest has ripped the mouse mask up that has sat untouched in the piano stool for the best part of five years)... or a character out of the Midnight Gang (definitely easier as just pyjamas and a bandage round his head... although no bandage as it was used on the dog's leg a few years ago, so it would have been a recycled muslin cloth which she assured her son had been washed since anyone spewed on it)... No, her boys both decided they'd go as Spiderman.

Daddy pointed out that Spiderman wasn't even a book... Mummy quite frankly did not care one iota as anything that saved an evening of her life had got to be a bonus and at any rate, she thought there had probably been a comic book about Spiderman at some point in the history of the universe...

IT WAS 9pm on a Wednesday night. Mummy had already finished work for the week.

The next morning, Mummy was going for a few days' jaunt to España (actually in reality it would be a very civilised affair as Mummy was now rather pregnant and it looked like she was hiding a basketball under her top). At the time, Nana was prone to making helpful observations to Mummy that she had put on weight. Mummy mostly smiled graciously and chose not to say what was on her mind.

The key thing about this little trip was that Mummy was going alone, minus any offspring and minus her husband.

Mummy had been spurred on by Daddy, having had two golfing holidays on his own every year for the past three. She figured before the newest baby joined the gang, it was time for her to have a much needed catch-up with her dearest Spanish friend and a couple of days' immersion to resurrect her Spanish. Some twenty-four years ago, Mummy had lived in Spain and she'd left part of her heart there with the friends she had made.

She had given Daddy warning of this trip a full two months earlier and, thankfully, he had remembered and was ready for action. Kids were also ready for action as they had informed Mummy that part one of their plan was to take Daddy shopping to the local supermarket as he always bought lots of sweeties when Mummy was away. Mummy didn't care as long as she wasn't going to have to deal with the aftermath of the E number consumption. Mummy knew that Nana was also ready for action as Nana had forgotten that her son had been an adult for quite some time now and that he knew how to cook and look after his own offspring. So, the children would be more than looked after while Mummy was away for all of forty-eight hours.

Mummy reflected on the difference between her preparations and Daddy's.

By this stage Daddy had been packed for a full two weeks. Mummy still hadn't packed.

Mummy finished work, collected children, made the obligatory Wednesday night quick tea of beans on toast and ferried her kids to swimming, piano and tag rugby. Whilst waiting for the activities to finish, Mummy and Olly popped to the local supermarket to stock up on dog food and she deftly headed off her three-year-old's meltdown at the pass as he had eyed up a cartoon character teddy that he thought he should have (apparently always wanted although he had never mentioned it before ever...).

She had sorted out washing, done a further two loads of washing, made packed lunches for the following day, dug out a baby photo of her youngest ready for his class project (baby photos easy to find as they were all sat in a bag waiting for Mummy to finally put them into an album). Also prepared were the ingredients for eldest daughter who was about to embark on a series of after-school cooking classes which evidently required half the cooking to be done at home the night before.

Daddy had thankfully suggested a takeaway instead of Mummy having to cook that evening.

Mummy polished off her late tea, then sat down for five minutes before finally getting round to packing. Mummy woke up groggily at 11.30pm and took herself off to bed. Packing would have to wait...

THREE DAYS later, Mummy was back, like she had never been away. Daddy had done a good job of holding the fort. Mummy was glad to be back in her own bed; sitting in plazas, people-watching whilst supping a cool drink and catching up on missed years with her friend, a sweet memory.

4.30am and Mummy woke up to the face of her three-year-old who proceeded to ask her whether she got the animals out of his bed. She started wondering whether she was in some kind of surreal dream. She told him they were at the end of his bed under the blanket (wrongly assuming he meant his cuddly toys).

Three-year-old was now on the brink of having a meltdown, so frustrated was he that her foggy brain wasn't catching up with his train of thought. He then proceeded to ask, had she shaken the animals out when she changed the sheets... She suddenly thought... Animals... Bug beds... No bed bugs... and reassured him that he definitely hadn't got any bed bugs in his bed (and had never had to her knowledge). He returned to bed, content.

Breakfast time and Mummy asked him why he had been concerned about bed bugs. It slowly emerged that whilst Mummy was away for a few days and Daddy was doing bedtime duties, Daddy had taught them the bedtime rhyme, with a difference... "Goodnight, sleep tight, don't let the bed bugs rip your legs off..."

Mummy reassured her son that no bugs were going to do any maiming or leg ripping off in their house... Daddy, on the other hand, may not come off so lightly.

Chapter 4

April

April had hit with a bump. Sadly, Mummy had to say goodbye to her dear Charlie (aka "aged hound") as she had deteriorated quickly over the previous fortnight. Mummy and Daddy were very fond of this doggie as she had been with them since the outset of their relationship. Mummy had bought her after "just going to look" at cute Labrador puppies. That was sixteen years ago. Daddy had bonded with Charlie very quickly as not long after getting Charlie, Mummy had gone on holiday with a friend and Daddy had looked after the young pup at his flat. Mummy had spent a lovely week in Spain and Daddy had survived a week house-training a pup, who had gone with him to visit Nana and Grandad at the tail end of the week and had ended up dredging Grandad's fishpond for lily pads whilst simultaneously scaring all his prized fish. Mummy told herself that Charlie had lived a good life. Still, she found it awfully hard to close this chapter on her faithful friend.

Daddy decided that they all needed cheering up and with the end of the extension work looming and a non-functioning kitchen for a few days, he had booked a week away in Sussex at the start of the Easter holidays. Mummy was beyond excited at the prospect of a week surrounded by comfort rather than brick-dust. Normally they didn't go away for Easter as there was so much going on at home. Mummy remembered back to the previous year; they had met up with some of their local Church friends for a Good Friday walk, followed by a pack-up lunch at the Pastor's house. After the lunch, everyone had come together to have a time of remembering Good Friday and a communion, kids included. Everything had been quiet and the "wine" (which was actually berry flavoured juice of some kind) had been passed around. Everyone had retained their little cup of wine, which they were planning on drinking together after a prayer had been said. Just after the prayer and before everyone had drunk from their cups, as people quietly sat and reflected, Riley had piped up at the top of his little voice, "Cheers," and had knocked back his juice. Mummy had wanted the floor to swallow her up. The Pastor had fallen about laughing and everyone else had been left wondering whether Mummy and her husband were seasoned drinkers.

"Yes," Mummy thought, "Let's go away for Easter."

"DO NOT, under any circumstances (apart from the house being on fire or there being blood) wake me up tomorrow morning," Mummy warned Riley. "If you do wake up early, you are allowed to go downstairs, you don't need to ask me... but don't wake anyone else up either," she said for good measure.

It was 10pm and all four children were still wide awake and wired as the first day of the family holiday had been spent driving seven hours "down south" to a holiday home on some farmland, in the Sussex countryside, grouped with a number of other holiday homes.

Surprisingly the travelling day had started off rather well; no arguments and no Daddy tutting whilst looking at his watch. Mummy thought this may be because in addition to working thirty-five hours over four days in paid work, she had spent the fifth day checking that the two girls had packed appropriate clothing and repacking the completely inappropriate clothing the two boys had attempted to pack. She had used up the vegetable contents from the bottom of the fridge by slinging it all into a pan with some stock and making a surprisingly tasty soup. She had also packed all food, clothing, toys, games and sundry items for the week. Daddy, meanwhile, had completed his paid work, played golf until late the night before the holiday, proceeded to manage a "lie-in" until half an hour before the estimated time of departure and then packed his stuff in the remaining twenty minutes.

As the journey progressed, Daddy's holiday mood increasingly deteriorated as the children revved up. Boredom kicked in once the "who can be the first one to spot game" had been exhausted and "I spy" was a failure as Olly hadn't grasped that it had to be something you could see with your naked eye and not some random item that you once saw somewhere in passing. Three motorway stops later; after a lunchtime stop spent convincing Olly that it was just Keele Services and not where the family were going to spend their week's holiday, a third stop was enforced as one child announced that they were desperate for the toilet just after sailing past a service station. Given that they had just joined the M25 with no prospect of a further service any time soon and as roadworks rendered any hard shoulder or parking place completely inaccessible with strictly no stopping allowed, muttering, Daddy was forced to turn off and stop in the entrance of a disused factory on the edge of some housing estate as all four children emptied their bladder contents on front wheel of the car and Mummy hoped CCTV cameras were not in use. Anyhow, seven hours later destination was reached and lovely it was too.

The first proper holiday morning dawned and by 6:45am, Riley had woken Olly up and then Mummy to ask whether he could go downstairs. Mummy had begrudgingly got up, sorted sons out, ensured they were fed and watered, stuck them in front of the telly and gone back to bed. Upon being woken up for the fifth time, Mummy abandoned any hope of sleep and groggily descended into the lounge and through her grog surveyed the mess that had been created in the space of half an hour.

"Why is this here?" she asked offspring (son had woken all siblings up by this time) as she held up a stuffed sausage dog, having retrieved it from the middle of the floor.

Son piped up: "It's to keep the giraffes out."

"Giraffes?" Mummy questioned.

"Yes," said son, "Daddy said it keeps the giraffes out."

This was Sussex we were in, not the Serengeti... Mummy's brain began to engage... "draught, not giraffes!" said Mummy, pretty sure that there weren't marauding giraffes wandering around the Sussex coastline.

After a morning going swimming, arguing over Uno and running around the garden, a lunchtime walk into the neighbouring village ensued; children ate half their bodyweight in cake at the local café and everyone trundled back to the house in the drizzle as a week of unbroken Spring sunshine had given way to the standard British weather. Mummy promptly hid away and collapsed into glorious naptime while Daddy amused the children until late afternoon when the family got to explore the coastline. Unfortunately, heavy fog descended, obscuring breath-taking views. Olly relayed to the rest of the family that the seven "dwarves" could not be seen because it was too "froggy", which Daddy deciphered into not being able to see the Seven Sisters because of the fog.

Day was topped off, back at the accommodation, with Mummy introducing a game of "Ten sticks on a board" which started off well but descended into chaos as Nell got to the board, flicked them up and one of them hit Riley in the face. Olly then joined his brother, crying because he wanted to kick the board. Mummy, aware that Sussex neighbours may not be as long-suffering as Welsh neighbours, decided it was time to call it a day and have tea, which led to all four children crying loudly as they got back into the house. Mummy congratulated herself on single-handedly reducing her entire entourage of offspring to tears.

PRIOR TO the holiday, Daddy had suggested that they take the kids for a day's fishing. Daddy used to fish a lot, he used to take off for a full day, returning just before sunset. This particular type of day-out stopped when for the third time Daddy returned from such a day and found his wife stood with a positive pregnancy test in hand, like she was somehow punishing him for having had a day out.

Mummy looked upon fishing as an opportunity to sit in the great outdoors, listening to the water lapping gently on the side of the banks, wrapped up warm, supping a cuppa, with the occasional interesting bird calling, peace and quiet and a chance to catch up on reading. Oh wait... That was before children...

Post four children, the reality... made it to the fishing ponds without too many arguments, which was just as well as the children spent most of the five hours that ensued arguing about whose turn it was to fish alongside Daddy. Although Daddy actually spent a lot of the five hours going from one child to another helping them to sort their snagged lines out.

Mummy's opportunity to read was tempered with the ever-present possibility that Olly may just take a step too far and join the elusive brown trout and salmon in the pond. Two hours into it, kids started to realise why Mummy hadn't been particularly over-enthusiastic at Daddy's suggestion to go fishing. All lunch had been eaten and Riley had to be held back from tucking into the tiger loaf that Daddy had bought to ensnare the fish.

Thankfully, after what seemed an age, fish started to bite, despite the fact that Olly was, at one point, using the Keep-net as a makeshift guitar and obliterating any remote possibility of Peace and Quiet taking up residence at this particular pond.

Nell and Maisie caught their dad's fishing bug and had a successful afternoon catching fish, interrupted only once by their youngest brother falling headlong down the bank, saved by Mummy's swift response; grabbing his ankle and hauling him back up, upside down, inches before he hit the water and unceremoniously plonking him back on the bank the right way up.

Rain did actually hold off, fish did actually get caught, Mummy did eventually get some of her book read and Pooh sticks amused everyone for half an hour as they leant over a bridge covering the mini waterfall. So, all in all, a good day was had by all and Mummy and Daddy were hoping that the kids' appetite for going fishing had been temporarily satisfied and that the next morning would be the first in a week when Daddy would not be woken up by Olly appearing at his bedside, face inches from Daddy's, at stupid o'clock in the morning, asking whether today was a fishing day...

Unfortunately, Olly didn't understand that holidays meant that you did not have to get up at the crack of dawn. Mummy decided to appease him with milk and kids' TV with the laughable idea that she would then be able to return to bed. She was sat on the coffee table in the lounge, waiting for the kettle to boil, blearily trying to get the blasted TV to work, when she felt a wet sensation reach her undercarriage and realised that Threenager had decided to empty contents of drinks container all over the table that she was sitting on, thus enforcing full shower and clothes change for her and putting paid to any plans for a return to bed.

Fresh as a daisy, she looked at the time and realised she was going to be able to take advantage of the daily invitation from the owners of the cottages to attend the "Feeding of the animals", which upon their arrival, Mummy and Daddy had snorted at, thinking it would be far too early for their crew... "Who in their right mind would attend that at that unearthly hour?" Turns out, as Mummy met a further four bleary-eyed parents from surrounding cottages across the farm, that quite a few in their right mind had the same idea.

Animal feeding began, but the animals turned out to be most unenthusiastic about the prospect of eight pint-sized toddleresque humans about to enforce feeding upon them. Rabbits were playing ball and allowed themselves to be man-handled by well-intentioned toddlers. Muffin, the Guinea pig, took some coaxing as she clung for dear life to the furthest corner of the cage and was finally yanked from her peaceful slumber, with an additional half cage of straw and foisted upon a snotty-nosed kid. Chickens ran amok as they dodged their way through marauding toddlers. Sheep and goats decided to ignore little outstretched hands offering food and go for the full pail of pellets, sending toddlers flying at all angles. Ducks were released from their overnight wooden hut and literally ran for the hills, avoiding pond at all costs, whilst toddlers stood there throwing stale bread into an empty pond and ducks looked on with disdain thinking, "You can shove your stale bread where the sun don't shine". Upon realising that her own tiny human was not one of the aforementioned children throwing bread to the disinterested ducks, Mummy discovered the reason for this was because he had opted to eat the stale bread himself. She decided to abandon the animal-feeding debacle and instead go and attend to feeding of the ranks in her own cottage. All this before 7.45am on a holiday day...

The rest of the week flew by. Mummy planned and executed a mammoth Easter egg hunt... so whilst her youngest napped and her older ones were run ragged going upstairs, downstairs, outside and inside for what would easily take them half an hour, Mummy sat having some downtime and indulging in her art and a tincy wincy bit of chocolate.

Mummy and Daddy also took the children to a zoo on one of the days that it was better weather. Halfway round, Olly (whose first trip it was to the zoo), commented: "This is boring, all we are doing is looking at animals," at which Mummy simultaneously laughed and cried.

Driving back from their accommodation, Mummy and Daddy noticed that the road announcement signs were showing an amber warning for heavy rain and wondered about how correct these predictions were.

Very correct, it turned out... so, the following morning was spent dragging four children around a local town looking for indoor children's activities. Heavy rain became heavier, so Mummy invested in cheap umbrellas for everyone. Riley's umbrella broke within five minutes, so he walked around with an umbrella closing on his head. What Mummy hadn't foreseen was that Olly had effectively been issued with a weapon of mass destruction as one three-year-old, desperately needing a nap, tired from walking around, was at knee height with everyone else. Mummy could be seen holding the hand of a walking, talking umbrella and Olly was getting more and more disgruntled that everyone was getting in the way. Initially amused passers-by did not remain amused as this walking umbrella left indentations in knees and nether regions. All in all, an exhausting morning for everyone. Thankfully, the rain cleared later and an afternoon was spent on the beach having a stone-throwing competition into the sea.

Mummy and Daddy arrived home that weekend to a quiet house; no builders, no machines, hardly anything resembling rubble being left in the garden and a functioning kitchen and bathroom. Mummy was absolutely delighted at this discovery, as she had been finding that her nesting instinct was extremely incompatible with a building site for a home. Mummy ordered everyone to take their bags to their rooms and unpack, having learnt from previous experience that otherwise, everyone would descend into normality immediately and she would be left unpacking everyone's bags for a further week. She had much to be thankful for from this week and treasured the time she had spent with the family, even if at times she had wanted to tear her hair out.

Chapter 5
May

After having wiggled and waggled his wobbly tooth for about three weeks, refusing all offers from Daddy to tie a piece of string round it and attach it to the doorknob, the family were sat having their evening meal when Riley sucked up his spaghetti and realised that his tooth was missing... just like that... missing.

"Where's my tooth?" he shouted out... a frantic search ensued... floor, dinner plate... after having mistaken the third piece of melted cheese for his missing tooth, Daddy declared that he may well have swallowed it, mentioning that Tooth Fairy may have to check his undies. Riley was mortified. Mummy managed to console him and one hour later, Riley had settled down for the night with a note under his pillow for the tooth fairy explaining that he thought he had swallowed his tooth... Mummy, mentally reminded herself to remove note and replace with coin later. She had often forgotten with his older siblings (they have reached the age where Mummy can just tell them that the Tooth Fairy is having to wait until the end of the month as she is skint). At one stage Maisie had gone through a spate of many teeth falling out in quick succession. The Tooth Fairy wasn't sure whether Maisie actually possessed a little hammer that she was knocking them out with once she realised that teeth had a monetary value. That little episode had rendered the Tooth Fairy brassic and Daddy had pitched in.

Mummy was just about to depart from the boys' room when Olly's little voice piped up, "Mummy, I need a note too."

"Why?" asked Mummy

"Because I have a wobbly nose," said Olly.

Note was duly deposited under Olly's pillow. Mummy, stifling her giggles, explained that his nose was wobbly. Mummy wasn't quite sure who the note was for, or indeed what recompense should be given for a wobbly nose.

There had often been discussions about what the Tooth Fairy does with the teeth once she had gathered them. Unlike some mummies who kept the teeth in memory boxes, this Mummy, I mean, Tooth Fairy, recoiled at the idea of the teeth of four, soon to be five children, sitting in a box in the house... Why would you? So, teeth tended to be unceremoniously flushed down the toilet as soon as they had been collected, although Tooth Fairy did wait until the full flush had finished to ensure that the teeth had definitely disappeared; who knew what nightmares could have been triggered by finding floating teeth in the loo should one of the children have woken up in the middle of the night.

SCHOOL WAS back post Easter break. Included in the week's school newsletter was a handy little piece of advice about how to avoid lateness in school arrival times. The school had also developed a weekly league table of school years to say which year had the best attendance.

Mummy read through the list and mentally checked them off:

1. Set the Alarm Clock to allow you enough time to get everybody ready ✅

2. Prepare School Bag, PE Kit and Uniform the night before ✅

3. Ensure children have recommended nine-eleven hours' sleep each night ✅

4. Switch off all TVs, Tablets and Computers at least one hour before bedtime ✅

Mummy wondered whether the author of these handy snippets lived in a Faraway land with Laa-Laa, Dipsy and friends... Sweet Maria, if Mummy set the alarm clock any earlier then she may as well not bother going to blasted bed at all.

Uniforms WERE neatly laid out the night before but there was a void somewhere between upstairs and downstairs where odd items of uniform and school shoes disappeared in the five minutes it took Mummy to have a shower. Also, Mummy's offspring interpreted: "I want you dressed by the time I get out of the shower," as, "Empty the entire contents of your Lego box out onto the floor for Mummy to stand on."

Children did regularly get eleven-twelve hours of sleep each night and got up in plenty of time.

Screen time was limited anyway as screens of any description were used as bargaining tools for good behaviour / chore completion.

Mummy thought through a typical morning scenario that they obviously had no idea about. Nell would have been ready since time began, Maisie would be having a fashion meltdown, Riley would have gone upstairs to clean teeth and come downstairs having deposited what looked like the entire tube of toothpaste all over his uniform and for good measure wiped any remnants on the wall on his way down the stairs, Ollie would have gone upstairs fully clothed and when Mummy arrived upstairs to clean her teeth, he'd be found sitting butt naked playing with a wooden train track.

And then, after managing to finally get everyone to the car, Mummy would politely request that her four offspring get in the car, progressing to a whispered scream through clenched teeth accompanied by 'The Look', culminating in full sergeant major requests to get in the car. In fact, the neighbours thought that two of her children were called "Move it" and "Get in the car" so often it was that they heard this.

Just that morning, a fight had broken out between three of them about who was going to sit in the front / nearest the door as they had all wanted to hightail it out of the car at the school gates. Mummy had resorted to threatening she'd go without them and one of her offspring had embarked on Battle of Wills and thrown down the gauntlet for Mummy to "go without me then", as they calmly shut the door and returned to the garden. Mummy had revved the engine and pulled off like she was auditioning for a part in the Fast and the Furious as other offspring belatedly offered up their seats to the rebelling sibling who had long since returned to the back garden.

Mummy had driven all of ten metres and realised she couldn't possibly leave her child in the back garden all day so reversed and honked the horn as her mini-me (in more ways than one) returned to the car and the family sat in stony silence to school where they were spectacularly late, which meant Mummy had to drive into the school grounds and around the one way system to the drop-off zone, instead of throwing them out of the door at the entrance to the school grounds, resulting in having to queue with all the other spectacularly late parents for the drop-off zone where her youngest child refused point blank to be dropped off and walk the two metres to the school door on his own (as his older siblings had disappeared already). So, Mummy had to get out and smile encouragingly at him as she quickly, on tiptoes, grabbed him and shoved him through the front door of school (not sure why tiptoes... thought they communicated a sense of apology to other parents that she knew she was holding everyone up but c'est la vie as she couldn't very well leave her child on the path).

Mummy had completed her walk of shame back to the car in the drop-off zone, kept her eyes down and joined the queue of other parents as she had spent the next 20 minutes trying to get out of the school grounds.

AS MUMMY was getting ever more pregnant and now could not face the prospect of supermarket shopping, she had decided to trial 'Click and Collect' at her local supermarket instead. Unfortunately, the 'Click and Collect' service appeared to have morphed into a 'Click and Hope for the Best' service, coupled with a parental training exercise in 'how to keep your cool whilst a car full of hungry children scream/cry/hit each other/wind each other up/pick their nose and eat it' (delete as appropriate).

One Sunday, on the way back from church, Mummy had been waiting for a good five minutes for someone to answer the intercom. She made the decision to hurry things along by locking the car, instructing her eldest to hold the fort and running (as best she could in this latest trimester of pregnancy) to Customer Services, hurriedly explaining her predicament and running (using the term loosely) toot sweet back to the rabble in the now rocking car...FIFTEEN minutes later there was still no sign of life from the back end of the store delivery section. Mummy rang Customer Services again and explained she had now been waiting for twenty-five minutes... The customer services person helpfully remembered the name of the harassed woman she had dealt with fifteen minutes earlier and told Mummy the reason for the delay was because the lady covering home shopping had gone for her lunch.

Let's say that by this stage Mummy's response was less than understanding and cheerful. Mummy did get home eventually with delivery finally in the rear of the car, to find they had missed off a couple of items and substituted an iceberg lettuce with spring onions, which only served to remind Mummy why she abandoned having home deliveries in the first place; substitutions for goods that weren't available was akin to Russian roulette... at one stage fabric conditioner had been substituted with whisky... say no more.

FRIDAY, DADDY agreed to go and collect Nell and Maisie from their Friday night kids' club. Riley and Olly begged Daddy to go too, so he relented and Mummy had a surprise half an hour to herself while Daddy disappeared with the clan. Mummy suspected that Riley and Olly had an ulterior motive, as enroute to the kids' club was a sweetie-laden supermarket and Daddy was partial to a sweetie or two.

The following day, Mummy and Nana took the kids for a trip out to the neighbouring town. Nana was treating them all to lunch after a shopping trip. On the way back from the shopping trip they passed a cyclist who was lying in the road, being helped by a number of passing motorists. They could see that he was being helped, so Mummy made the decision not to stop and to drive on.

Mummy was surprised to receive a phone call the following Monday evening, from her friend who had been helping with the Sunday kids' service at Church the day before. Evidently, during the kids' session, Maisie had announced to everyone that Mummy had hit a pedestrian and kept on driving.

Mystified, Mummy relayed this to her husband and found out that on his drive home from picking them up from Friday kids' club, a pigeon had hit the roof of a 4x4 in front of them, rolled off the roof (dead) and had disappeared under the car causing Daddy to drive with a great 'ploof' of feathers. Kids had thought it was hilarious (Mummy was slightly worried about this).

Mummy resolved to explain to her daughter the difference between the words "pigeon" and "pedestrian" and also made a mental note to speak to the leaders of the Sunday kids' team, to ensure that they understood it was a pigeon, not a pedestrian, lest they started to think that Mummy and Daddy were the new Bonnie and Clyde of North Wales; Mummy heartlessly mowing down a pedestrian and driving nonchalantly on, leaving a trail of destruction in her path in readiness for Daddy to drop them his business card.

Chapter 6

June

As Mummy's due date was drawing ever closer, her midwife suggested that the next appointment was with the Consultant, Mr Peters, who incidentally was a dead-ringer for a comedian off the telly which led to a confused Mummy the first time she met him, as she was convinced she had just watched him on a panel show the evening before and wondered how on earth he was managing to moonlight given he had such a responsible job. On that occasion, Mummy and Daddy had turned up at the hospital with Mummy, forty-one weeks pregnant and the receptionist had smiled and told her Mr Peters would work his magic.

"His magic" had been a rather painful sweep, but, lo and behold, one baby had arrived within twenty-four hours and so it had continued. Now that this was her fifth pregnancy, Mr Peters and Mummy went back a long way. Mr Peters had also met Daddy a few times, normally when he had his hand halfway up Mummy's jacksy. Mr Peters had "worked his magic" on two more of her past pregnancies, as her babies seemed to like to hang on in there and stayed well beyond their due dates. This time, Mr Peters explained that because of her age, the risks were higher for Mummy and eventually a compromise was reached, as Mummy did not want to be induced. Mummy reminded Mr Peters that his previous advice was that induction increased the risk of intervention by seventy per cent. Mr Peters would start with "sweeps" at thirty-eight weeks and there would be daily monitoring after the due date. Mummy knew that ultimately this baby would come when it came and no amount of sweeps would help. Likewise, her birth plan was thrown out of the window during her first labour and she had come to realise that you could have all kinds of wonderful plans, but ultimately a baby's safe arrival is the most important thing, so plans may go awry.

Thirty-eight weeks arrived. Mummy attended on her own as Daddy was conducting a funeral. Mr Peters was accompanied by a female assistant. Mr Peters made enquiries as to how Daddy was, which led him on to discussing ancient Chinese burial techniques. Mummy was somewhat taken aback that it was at the precise moment of performing a sweep that Mr Peters was discussing burial chambers, hoping that it was not the task in hand that had triggered this conversation. Assistant nurse was also somewhat confused that this should be the topic of conversation, obviously not knowing the context of Daddy's job and the fact that Mummy and Daddy knew Mr Peters due to having met up in a professional capacity every now and then over the past thirteen years.

Thirty-nine weeks came and went. Nothing... "Carry on as usual," thought Mummy.

DINNERTIME CONVERSATION after church; Olly enquired as to whether Mummy had seen the machetes outside on the grass?

Mummy wracked her brains, admittedly she was rather tired and her powers of observation may not have been quite as sharp as usual, but she felt sure she would have noticed weaponry lying about next to the cheerful Summer Planters on her way in...

"Machetes?" she double checks...

"Yes... machetes..." her youngest son repeated and then, for clarification, added... "You know... they throw them at weddings..."

"Ahhh... you mean confetti?" Mummy was very glad to have cleared that one up. It could be a very messy business throwing machetes at a wedding.

"Anyway, what was Sunday kids about this morning?" she asked.

Olly: "He had bubbles and set fire to them and didn't burn his hands and some went on the carpet." Mummy is not sure where this is going...

Nell: "There were three men."

Riley (interrupting Nell): "A Scottish man." Mummy thought this sounded like the beginning of a joke as she didn't entirely recollect there being a Scotsman in her Bible.

Maisie: "No, a Bendy Goat and I've forgot the other names."

The penny dropped... "Do you mean Shadrach, Meshach and Abednigo?" Mummy asked.

"Yes!" they all shouted.

Mummy inwardly resolved to ensure that she re-visited some of those bits of the Bible as only last week, Maisie had reported that they had been learning all about Moses who arrived in the desert in a helicopter.

SPORTS DAY... Was it just Mummy or was sports day taking place earlier and earlier each year? She normally had to squeeze it into a lunchbreak from work, but now that she was on maternity leave, she had the luxury of time (although to be honest, she would rather not spend this time sitting in the middle of a field at the mercy of the inclement weather that constitutes British Summertime). Sports day had advanced significantly since her day, Mummy thought; a ragged old sack, jumping for all you were worth and falling over at every jump. Now we had full track and field events and a P.A. system rigged up to Mr Rhys' car battery (battery still firmly in the car engine, bonnet raised). Music played while the teachers organised the children, which was more akin to herding goats. Riley was boogying with abandon to the music, while he waited for the races to start, oblivious to the one-hundred-plus onlookers. Mummy had remembered to bring her camping chair to sit on and sat amidst the other parents.

Daddy could, unfortunately, not get time off as work was rather busy. Daddy had received a few random phone calls at work lately. A few days earlier, he received a call from someone who had got a wrong number.

Daddy: "Hello, Robinson's Funeral Services."

Caller: "I am ringing to book an eye test."

Daddy: "I think you have the wrong number, however if you were to book an appointment with me, I can guarantee you that one hundred per cent of the people who come here never have trouble with their eyesight again."

The races had begun. Every school year doing four races each. "We could be here a while," thought Mummy, hoping that baby number five didn't decide to make an entrance on the school field.

Thankfully, clouds had parted and the sun had broken through. The children all did well. The school gave everyone a prize whether they were first, last or somewhere in between. Mummy particularly enjoyed watching one of Riley's classmates method of tackling the obstacle race; started off attempting to balance a beanbag on his curly mop of hair, gave up after it had fallen off twice and went with the 'hold on to it firmly hope none of the seven teachers and one hundred parents notice and run' method, ended by flinging it into the awaiting hoop, himself following through the hoop... Then on to egg and spoon, which was going well, but upon it falling off for the fifth time, he gave in and drop-kicked it to the sack. Riley, on the other hand, just firmly held onto his "egg" with his thumb. Classmate, unlike three of the other kids in the race, managed to get the sack up to his knees and then, clinging on for dear life, jumped as hard as he could towards the finishing line. Realising he stood a good chance of gaining third position in the race, he reached to within a body's length of the finishing line, by which time the sack had worked its way down to his ankles and then he just aimed and unceremoniously fell head-long across the finishing line. For effort and comic effect, he won. Mummy cheered.

Mummy reflected that the silver-lining of being thirty-nine weeks pregnant was that you have a legitimate excuse for not taking part in the parents' race at the end of the sports day. It's that race where everyone tries to pretend that they are just doing it for fun, but then there's that one parent who suddenly unleashes her competitive streak (she has already posted on social media that morning what her pre-race macro-full breakfast is) and so, despite your best efforts to pretend to be nonchalant, you want to try and whoop them all in the race.

WEEK FORTY. Still no sign of Baby #5 despite lots of hot curry, fresh pineapple and walking. Mummy had now given up carefully measuring out Gaviscon on a spoon and was swigging it like it was going out of fashion. Daddy observed that Mummy looked like a wino swigging whisky. Mummy didn't care, she had a bottle in her pocket, a bottle in her bag and a bottle by the side of the bed.

Braxton Hicks were regularly starting but they got to three minutes apart and then Mummy would fall asleep and wake up in the morning still pregnant. On two occasions this particular week they had been so convincing, that Opa had been called and Daddy had driven Mummy to the hospital in the middle of the night, they'd been offered a cuppa and then contractions had stopped. Daddy said that the midwives were going to start thinking they just liked a cheap night out; a bit of a drive to the local hospital and a cuppa courtesy of the NHS.

In the light of there still being no baby, Mummy preferred to continue with normality for as long as possible, so despite her boys trying to do their very best at persuading her to temporarily suspend piano lessons, Mummy insisted that they continue. Admittedly, Friday afternoon was probably not the best time for Olly (having just turned four) to have a piano lesson, albeit ten minutes only.

Piano teacher turned up in a good mood. "Have you been practicing?" he asked Olly. "Yes," said Olly (Mummy had threatened him with no snack/drink/screen time if he didn't practice first that day, but apart from that, his practice has been wanting).

Olly started off well but insisted on playing the rests. Piano teacher started to get a tad frustrated, trying unsuccessfully to explain not to play the rests. In the end, he said, "Tell you what, just say it... Fish and chips... (REST)... Fish and chips... (REST)... I... (REST)... Like... (REST)... Fish and chips."

Olly said it and played it at the same time (still playing the rests).

Irate piano teacher said: "No, just say it to begin with, don't play it."

Olly did as he was told, then suggested, "We could say... Ca rrot head (rest), Ca rrot head (rest), You are a Ca rrot head."

Mummy (who was stood in the now-adjoining kitchen listening) heard frustrated teacher suggest we stick to the script.

Olly decided to comply and quietly played piano so you could barely hear it. Piano teacher demonstrated how to play the keys so you could hear it. Son looked at teacher and said: "You're not allowed to play it that hard, you'll wreck the piano."

Mummy stifled a laugh as she thought how this sounded like something she would say.

Olly asked: "Is it time to go now?" Mummy thought piano teacher wished it was. Olly decided to give piano teacher rendition of 'Dude is like a lady... Yeah... Yeah... Dude is like a lady' at which point Mummy decided to rescue afflicted piano teacher and told Olly to behave.

End of lesson couldn't come soon enough... Piano teacher breathed out as he steeled himself for next twenty minutes with Mummy's third youngest offspring. Riley's lesson passed without a hitch. Piano teacher told him: "I would like you to practice that every day and not let anything stop you."

Riley: "What about if the house is on fire?"

Mummy muffled a guffaw and thought piano teacher had the patience of a saint.

AS MUMMY was no longer in the mood or position to do any major exercise, the children were also not getting much exercise either, so, in an attempt to get them away from screens this week and also to make the most of the light nights and extremely sunny weather, Mummy decided to reintroduce badminton in the front garden. Mummy's idea was children frolicking in the garden on a sunny afternoon. Mummy's reality, on the other hand, was children wanting to play it at seven o'clock in the morning in the garden. Mummy refused until 7.45am with threats that any noise at all and they would be back inside, as all the neighbours were still sleeping.

Mummy went upstairs to get ready and emerged from the shower to hear three of her four offspring whisper-arguing. She went to the window to see what was going on, only to catch one child whacking the other one with a badminton racket whilst the other retaliated by thwacking them back. Shuttlecock was well and truly abandoned as one thwacked child burst into loud yells and the third child, oblivious to the wounding and maiming going on, complained at the top of their voice that they hadn't had a go. Mummy knocked on the window with her most ferocious face on and mouthed: "Get your backsides back inside now."

Harmonious sporting activity ideals were abandoned as Mummy inwardly apologised to neighbours for the early morning wake-up call of squawking children.

As they sat down for breakfast, the discussion turned to loving your neighbour and loving others as we would like to be loved, which was apt, Mummy thought.

Five minutes later, Maisie disappeared to relieve herself and her parting words to her younger brothers were, "Don't come in the bathroom or I'll batter you..."

Mummy sighed; she was obviously going to have to revisit this one. The boys were given a quick lesson in 'irony'.

Chapter 7

July

Due date had come... and gone. True to her word, Mummy honoured her agreement with Mr Peters, her consultant and she had been attending the hospital daily for monitoring of the baby. Mummy had also now had four sweeps, but this baby was hanging on in.

The advantage of heading up to the hospital every night was that Daddy was left to run the gauntlet of bedtime. Mummy had quickly discovered that daytime at the hospital was no good, as she had fat chance and no chance of finding the holy grail that was a parking space anywhere near where she needed to be, meaning a long walk, which she knew was good, but was also more of a waddle at this stage, adding to the complication that she had a baby jumping on her bladder most of the time by then.

Mummy also had a friend who worked in the maternity unit, who brought her a cup of tea, so she was able to read her book, enjoy a hot cup of tea and put her feet up for an hour or so, which was bliss, except that before entering the ward, she had to sit in the waiting room, which happened to be next door to a delivery suite. Mummy wondered whether the sounds emanating from the delivery suite were anything like the sounds she emitted when she was in full-blown labour. Having had four babies, Mummy had a way of tackling labour, which was to get into a kind of zone. Daddy was also, surprisingly, quite good at labour, although given half a chance he would have opted for not being there at all, as it turned his stomach, he'd said. "Turns your stomach???" Mummy had given Daddy that look and he had been silenced.

Daddy and Mummy had worked well as a team during labour. He had passed her the sick-bowl and had fought her corner if the midwives had come up with any fandangled ideas that had not been what Mummy had wanted. He had been there, but hadn't fussed her, which is just what Mummy had needed when she had been in this zone. Daddy knew his wife well. Daddy's game plan for labour was "Stick to the end that eats, otherwise it is like watching your favourite pub burn down."

Mummy and Daddy had both had a tour of the midwifery-led unit a few weeks previously and Mummy had thought, as this was her last pregnancy, that she would love to be in a less sterile setting; She saw the soft-lighting and the Bluetooth-enabled birth-pool so you could play your choice of music. Daddy saw the television and thought he could watch the golf while his wife gave birth. Mummy thought she would shove a golf club where the sun doesn't shine should this happen.

Mummy was bone-tired but could not sleep. She had only just finished for maternity leave a week previously and had the sum-total of four hours sleep a night. She was either awake needing the loo, or her acrobatic baby was getting going the minute she lay down. She had a nervous energy of being overdue, wondering whether each night was THE night, alongside making sure that if anything happened in the night, she had fully prepared everything for the next day so that her other children were catered for. Mummy wondered whether it was nature's way of getting her ready for no-sleep when the baby was born.

Forty-one weeks – This night, as Mummy was waiting at the hospital with a particularly noisy birth going on in the neighbouring room, she felt a contraction and then another. She agreed with the midwife that she would go home and come back in the morning as she was feeling rather uncomfortable and it looked like it would be a while before she was brought onto the ward for monitoring.

Back home, when the contractions were three minutes apart, Daddy suggested they ring Opa again. Mummy was blasé as these three-minute apart contractions had happened a number of times in the past two weeks and ended in nothing. She finished folding the washing and grabbed her bag. Daddy asked her to hang fire on having the baby as he didn't want it to arrive enroute to the hospital. The last two babies that Mummy and Daddy have had made very quick appearances. Mummy was not in the mood to be told where to give birth.

Two and a half hours later, Baby number five arrived without any fuss, in the pool, as Mummy had wanted. Miss Isla was adorable. Daddy went home for a few hours' sleep before the rabble were wakened. Mummy had tea and toast and cuddles and Isla was checked over. Daddy returned later that day to collect Mummy and Isla.

UNLIKE ROYALTY, who emerge from the hospital a mere seven hours after having given birth, looking radiant and stunning, walking in heels... Mummy's post-partum version of herself was not quite so slick.

Mummy emerged from hospital gingerly, having collected her dignity, which she had left alongside her pelvic floor, somewhere near the entrance to the hospital on her way in. As she was trailing behind her six-foot-two tall husband who had forgotten that his wife had just birthed a baby and was, therefore, not up for sprinting (also she was not blessed with long legs). Baby Isla was being carried in car seat by Daddy.

Mummy had dark rings under her eyes due to the all-nighter she had just pulled giving birth. This time she had avoided the hell of the postnatal ward where you just manage to get your new, tiny human off to sleep and someone else's tiny human starts squealing and wakes yours up again and you slowly realise that a good night's sleep is a thing of the past, at least for the next three years or so.

MUMMY WAS still waddling around in maternity trousers which concealed three industrial-sized hospital pads as her nether regions attempted to reassemble themselves two weeks later. On a trip into town, Olly enquired as to why she was wearing a nappy (at the top of his voice in the middle of the Town Hall public toilets). She heard a muffled snigger from the person in the cubicle next door. Mummy had quietly resigned herself to the fact that bouncing on a trampoline was probably a thing of the past.

The midwife had recommended "Spritz for bits" which was a whole lot easier than the last time round, when Mummy had been told to put witch hazel on the wounds; all well and good should she have ever managed to get past the stomach that she still had and contort herself into that position without putting her back out permanently. Back then, Mummy had resorted to a mirror down below helping her to aim witch hazel in the general direction of pain but getting more of it on the bathroom floor than the intended target.

Gradually, Mummy began to feel more normal and a routine was quickly established as Daddy had to return to work. Mummy couldn't quite believe that the school holidays were almost upon them and she was feeling about as revved up about this as a turkey waiting for Christmas. Mummy was under no illusions that the approaching summer was going to be a tasking one with a newborn in tow. Mummy felt like she could fall asleep on a washing line, so wondered how she was going to handle amusing five children for six weeks.

As the final day of term loomed, Opa decided to gift the children a game for their amusement over the summer. This tied in nicely with Mummy's plans to restrict screentime to an hour a day so that the kids could do something other than watch gumph on screens. Actually, Opa had been having a clear out and before taking it to the recycling yard, he called round to see if Mummy could make use of it.

Riley and Olly's eyes lit up when they caught sight of Opa stood at the back gate with a croquet set and Mummy agreed to take it as it was still in perfectly good condition. She was about to deposit it amidst the other rammel in the shed when her boys asked whether they could use it. Mummy agreed, instructed them to take it to the front garden and told them they'd have to ask Daddy to look up "How to play croquet" on YouTube.

Boys took off to the front garden and looked like they were doing it right in terms of setting it out, so Mummy returned to clearing up the remnants of supper. No sooner had she done this, she could hear Daddy's not so dulcet tones shouting, "No!" as he hammered on the window.

Mummy ran to find out what the commotion was in time to catch the tail end of one of her sons bringing down his mallet with all the finesse of Tiger Woods as he swung it like a golf club towards the croquet ball, missed and sent a good wedge of grass flying high into the air. Mummy quickly had words as she envisaged croquet balls heading towards their lounge window very soon otherwise.

Riley came inside to briefly have the general idea of the game explained to him, but this appeared to have gone in one ear and out of the other when he returned to front garden where he and Olly used the mallets as makeshift crutches, weapons and the metal hoops were draped over ears as earrings.

Mummy managed to get them to agree that maybe they should put it away until she had time to read up on the rules and how to play properly. Meanwhile, the front lawn had already been hacked to within an inch of its life and, "The boys are out playing croquet on the lawn", was not quite as serene as it might sound as croquet mallets had very nearly become weapons of mass destruction in the hands of her young sons.

THE FINAL day of term arrived. Having four children in primary school/pre-school and two of them having teaching assistants or teachers, could potentially lead to an expensive affair when it came to teachers' end of term gifts. Mummy remembered being in primary school and was pretty sure they never gave any gifts to the teachers at the end of term. Where this tradition had come from, she had no idea. A few years before, she had the brainwave that rather than spend half a mortgage on teachers' and teaching assistants' gifts, she would rustle up a tray of chocolate brownies and put them into little bags for her children to distribute. This had worked extremely well and everyone was happy... although there had been one year when Maisie emerged with an empty bag of what had been brownies and explained that her teacher had said that she could eat the brownies herself. Mummy had not been convinced.

This year, Mummy collected four very excited children from school and nursery and along with Baby Isla, they went for an end of term treat to their favourite ice cream parlour, where they spent a good half an hour deciding which flavour combinations to have.

Chapter 8

August

The first few weeks of the summer holidays were a haze. Mummy felt like she had a permanent hangover without the aid of alcohol... a sleep-deprivation hangover. It never failed to amaze Mummy that she could go from a fully-functioning, sociable, responsible manager at work, to someone whose sole focus, at least for the first six weeks of newborn-ness, was feeding, bowel movements and what colour those movements were. A day was dominated by routines; feeds, sleeps, poos and guilt... guilt that she felt too exhausted to amuse her other kids. Guilt when she dared to have a glimpse at her social media feed and found it full of people sunning themselves in far-off climates, or organising rock-climbing in the morning, swimming in the afternoon and paddle-boarding in the evening, followed by fish and chips and a sunset. Mummy felt like she was just about surviving each day. Only a few weeks in and if Mummy heard a cry, she gauged it on her internal squeal thermometer to assess whether it really warranted her intervention, or whether she could continue attempting to drink the one hot drink of the day that hadn't been re-heated five times in the microwave.

August arrived and Mummy packed her daughters off to camp for a few days. The boys were most upset that they were not old enough to go and asked Mummy whether they could go camping too. Mummy thought back to the previous year...

Mummy and Daddy had wrongly assumed that camping with small children would be much simpler than a hotel holiday; they just needed a tent and some clothes and things to cook in a pan, right? It had been a while since they had been camping, admittedly, but if Steph could manage it every weekend with her one child and a dog, then surely two adults could manage four kids and two dogs? (That year, Mummy had been looking after her sister's hound as well as her own.) The campsite had been championing eco-friendly loos and had whole sections of bee-friendly areas and neighboured a farm, so Mummy and Daddy had thought the kids would be sure to enjoy looking at the animals.

The first mistake had been bringing the dogs. Mistakenly, they had thought they could contain the dogs in the foyer of the tent... but the first night put paid to that idea as the dogs had burrowed under and out. All the kids had finally been asleep and Mummy and Daddy had been sat enjoying a quiet drink, attempting to finally get into the mode of relaxed holiday, when out had popped Charlie, the labrador, closely followed by Finn (the retriever). Mummy had managed to grab the leads and attach them to the dogs but had failed to spot a fellow camper having a late-night wander with his two Rottweilers. Charlie and Finn, however, had spotted them and before Mummy could do anything about it, she had been dragged unceremoniously, hanging on to two leads, across the muddy field towards two large Rotties; Mummy looking like a crap water skier. Meanwhile, Daddy, rather than helping her, was sitting there, laughing at her and laughing even more when the gent had called after one of his Rotties to whom he had only gone and given the same name as Mummy. To say Daddy had been helpless with laughter would be an understatement. The hounds ended up having to be confined to the car (with the window ajar) but then every time some poor unsuspecting fellow camper emerged from a tent to go to the toilet block, Charlie and Finn had popped their heads up from slumber and had started barking. By 5am, as the sun was on its way up, Mummy had dragged them off for an impromptu walk across the fields to try and tire them out and stop them from barking.

It had rained on and off for the first three days; everything had been wet. Everything had smelt of wet dog. The midges had been driving Daddy so insane that each evening he could be found sitting there, zipped up to the eyeballs in his coat, with a can of bug spray in hand ready to blitz them. For two nights Daddy had woken Mummy up, dreaming that he had been on the edge of a cliff, clinging on to her. Mummy and Daddy had finally established that this dream was due to the tent being on a slope, but after the faff of putting it up, hadn't wanted to take it down so soon.

The kids had been up at the crack of dawn (literally) every morning, partly through excitement and partly because Mummy and Daddy didn't possess blackout compartments for the tent, so the minute any hint of daylight hit then the kids had been rising and shining. Mummy and Daddy were neither rising nor shining, apart from the morning, despite being told not to, when all the kids had got up quietly and had decided to let them have a lie-in. Mummy and Daddy had been woken by excited giggles and splashing and Nell had run back to inform them that they had found a stream to play in... cue one – Mummy hot footing it out of the tent in her pjs to find out where this stream had sprung from as it sure as heck hadn't been there the day before.

The "stream" (Mummy used the term loosely) had turned out to be the remnants of the eco-friendly loo that had flooded with the rainfall, so her dear cherubs had been delightedly paddling in watered-down sewage. At this point, Mummy had drawn the line and insisted they pack up and go home, but as they had been trying to pack up tents and all of their gumph along with four kids running around and two dogs looking for an opportunity to escape, Charlie, the lab, had managed to disappear across the field and after a good ten minutes calling for her (she always did have selective hearing, much like the rest of the family), she had emerged from a neighbouring tent carrying a half-eaten bag of sandwiches that she had half-inched.

So, this year, when the boys asked Mummy whether they could go camping, Mummy thought about that request for a nano-second before deciding she would rather stick pins in her eyes. She suggested, instead, a tent in the back garden but when it came down to it, it was raining, so the boys were more than happy with a pop-up tent and a midnight (actually 9pm) feast in their bedroom.

Since camping was out of the question, Mummy and Daddy had asked Opa whether they could borrow his static caravan for a week, which was only an hour away and just about big enough for them all. As soon as Mummy and Daddy crossed the bridge onto Anglesey, Mummy felt weights lift and lightness descend. She was actually quite excited at being away from her usual four walls as she realised just how isolating having a newborn could be in those early days and with it being the summer holidays, the usual Mummy groups weren't on. She had been craving adult conversation.

Upon arriving, the kids were so excited and careered up and down the caravan, in and out of the rooms and Olly spotted the wild rabbits outside and started chasing them around under the caravan. There was a neighbouring field of nosy cows who popped their heads over the fence to see who it was that had just turned up.

Daddy and the kids had been shopping for essential food items to take with them and had come back with milk, bread, loo paper and half a tonne of sweets and biscuits. Mummy was now regretting having given in and allowing the kids to have some sweets as a treat after their tea, as they were supposed to be asleep but were giggling and banging the wall in sugar-induced high spirits an hour after having been sent to bed. That said, Mummy was still glad of this time with her family.

Roll forward to the early hours of the morning with one screaming wet baby plus one pitch black caravan plus trying to find a dry baby-gro and change screaming, wet baby and do up a million poppers in the pitch black without waking the rest of the sleeping inhabitants of caravan... What have you got? One Mummy possessed and a new Olympic sport emerging. Mummy had to remind herself that this was a good idea.

The next day, they bundled into the car to go on one of their favourite family walks – The Red Squirrel walk – in search of the ever-elusive Red Squirrels. There were feeders strategically placed by the car park amongst the toweringly tall pine trees. This day, there were also many serious-looking Red Squirrel spotters, patiently waiting for a glimpse; one man even fully clad in camouflage gear with expensive cameras adorning his chubby neck. Imagine their delight when a clapped-out Zafira rocked up, diesel engine straining and the Clampetts got out (aka Mummy's delightful family).

Despite explaining to four-year-old that he needed to be quiet to see any squirrels, excitement overtook and with all the finesse of a Sergeant Major, his voice bellowed "Squirrels" and then the cry echoed from tree-top to tree-top around the forest with a ricochet effect ensuring that any Red Squirrel even toying with the idea of nipping down for a nut, thought better of it and headed for the hills; a mass exodus of red squirrels nearly getting run over as they vacated the forest over the busy A-road as Mummy, Daddy and clan continued to traipse round the forest. They all enjoyed their squirrel-less walk; stopping to pick early blackberries and finding tiny froglets hopping all over the forest to the lake in the middle. Mummy drank in the woodland air and sat down to look up and marvel at the way the light hit the leaves of the trees and the dappling effect it created on the ground. This was soul-food for Mummy; sitting under century-old trees, feeling small and thinking on the enormity of her Maker who had made all these beautiful things, who is vast, but also so interested in the intricacies of His children that He knew in this moment right here, she would be sitting drinking it in, revelling in His handiwork, refreshing her soul.

She had Baby Isla on her front, fast asleep, the kids stopped and played in the make-shift den that someone had created out of fallen logs in the clearing, Daddy had his camera out and took some really great shots of trees and flowers. Mummy loved the way Daddy could look at something and where someone else saw the obvious, he saw the untapped potential and his creativity brought something astounding out of the ordinary. It was a gift that Daddy had which had led to their home being full of an eclectic mix of old furniture, revamped and restored by Daddy.

Apart from the lack of squirrels, the walk was a success. To conclude the outing, Mummy and Daddy promised a stop at their favourite café which was so small that when they all piled in too, it was like meeting up with old friends as everyone chatted to everyone else in the café. They did the best hot chocolates, so in spite of it being the height of summer, the day was topped off by hot chocolate, cream and marshmallows.

Later, before she hit the sack herself, Mummy peeked in on her sleeping kids and she realised how blessed she was for this tribe who simultaneously brought chaos and fun into her life. Her heart felt full.

The week passed far too quickly. Ice-cream and coffee featured heavily. They had a tour round a castle, went in search of a hidden waterfall, had a few dalliances with soft play centres and farm parks and the final day of the holiday was beautiful, so they headed off to the beach with their slightly too tight wet-suits (except Mummy as alas, her post-partum body meant that her normal wetsuit didn't even get past her thighs at this stage). Bodyboards in hand they spent an afternoon body-surfing the waves, building sandcastles and finding interesting shells. As the tide came in, they had a stone-throwing competition, which had become a bit of a family tradition whenever they were near water.

BACK AT home, Mummy used the final week to ensure that all uniforms were sorted for school which was only seven days away. She had been putting it off but the inevitable day of needing to do the school-shoe shopping arrived. This was no mean feat (no pun intended) with five small children.

After the obligatory extra half hour necessary to get out of the door, they hit the town. Baby Isla had conveniently fallen asleep, something which Mummy was extremely glad about as half the battle was already won... all going according to plan, Mummy thought.

The minute they rocked up in town, youngest daughter woke up, which was not good as she has a distinct dislike of being in a car-seat/pushchair or any other combination of the two. So, Mummy proceeded to walk with one squealing baby and four older kids through the town centre. Resisting the urge to run back to the car, she soldiered bravely on.

The shoe shop was a sea of kids and parents, so they had implemented a ticket system. Mummy knew it didn't look good when they were allocated customer place number ninety-eight and it was only number ninety-four. Squealing daughter was still squealing, whilst everyone gave "Aww bless her" looks. Funny how that soon changed once they lost the new-born look and then everyone just looked with annoyance, willing you to sort out your screaming child.

At customer place ninety-six (they were getting there slowly) Olly sidled up to Mummy and uttered those words that filled every parent with dread... "Mummy, I need the toilet."

Mummy could not believe it, as exactly the same thing had happened school-shoe shopping the previous year... must be something about shoe shopping that set him off. "Can you wait?" Mummy asked, cautiously hopeful... no, he couldn't... "Right, come on," Mummy ordered the troops... "Quick."

They then set off at top speed, squealing child still squealing, Mummy deftly steered the pram through meandering shoppers... squealing child having same effect as emergency services, rather akin to a siren, as the way parted between shoppers. Mummy looked like a woman possessed with four kids flailing behind her. They commandeered the library's ladies' loos and then ran at top speed back to the shop just in time for their number to be called. Mummy congratulated herself. Mummy was also extremely happy that only one child needed new shoes, saving her the equivalent of half a mortgage.

Shoe shopping done, the trek back to the car had to take a diversion to the pram/bike shop as the pram got a flat tyre. Mummy offloaded bags onto the mini tribe of sherpas she had in tow whilst propping up the wonky pram at the same time as pushing it, with squealing baby in it. The man in pram shop took pity on Mummy and cleared the sofa for them to sit on. It was then, in a brief moment of quiet, that Mummy realised she had walked the entire way round town with baby puke all over her shoulder. "Classy,", Mummy thinks, "Classy."

DADDY ARRIVED home at the end of that week with a request for Mummy; One of Daddy's friends had purchased two puppies. There had been a change in their family and they were now having to look after three small grandchildren and didn't feel that they could manage two puppies as well. "Remember how you said that if we were to get another dog, it would be a little one that didn't moult?" Daddy reminded Mummy, "Well this one is little and doesn't moult."

Now Daddy knew that Mummy had a weak spot for waifs and strays. One year, Mummy had found a little dog sitting on the corner of their street when she popped home from work for lunch. She had never seen this dog before and as he had no tag on his collar, she thought she had better take him down to the local Police station, which she happened to be passing on her way back to work. Imagine her surprise when she returned home that evening to said little dog sitting back on the corner of their street. She had relayed this to Daddy at the time and Daddy had looked at her incredulously and then informed her that she had actually rescued the little dog from sitting outside his own house and that he belonged to the people who lived there. In her defence, the dog hadn't been there long. Daddy has teased her ever since.

Mummy made enquiries with Daddy as to what kind of dog it was and against her better judgement agreed that they could go and have a look at this pup.

PUP WAS adorable. All the children were instantly in love and Mummy couldn't very well say no now without being viewed as Cruella herself. Mummy was actually also very taken with George, as this pooch was already named. She had missed her dog-free days, she thought... conveniently forgetting just how easy it had been to up and off over the summer, well, apart from five children to organise. Daddy completely spoiled George who quickly established that Mummy was the boss, caregiver, food-giver and walker and Daddy was the pushover. Sixteen years of dog ownership and the rule had always been NO dogs upstairs in the house. Mummy could not believe Daddy was so besotted with newest pup that he suggested pup slept on his bed UPSTAIRS by his wife's side of the bed. Mummy went upstairs to get ready for bed and heard pitter-patter of tiny paws as Daddy had deposited pup and his bed upstairs. Hitherto zonked out pup now celebrated having ground new owner down and went nuts in sleeping sons' bedroom before christening hall carpet with poop (despite fact that Mummy had just stood outside with him in her dressing gown and slippers for the past fifteen minutes waiting for him to do what he needed to do... Instead, George had just sat there looking at her).

After scrubbing carpet clean, Mummy declared that this pup was staying downstairs as soon he wouldn't be quite so cutesie and poops would be a whole lot bigger too. "We shall start as we mean to go on, he is a dog, after all, not a child." As Daddy got gagging reflex at the mere thought of scrubbing turds out of the carpet, he had gone with Mummy's opinion for the time being.

Chapter 9
September

"Off they go" posted Mummy alongside obligatory back to school photo as she had cajoled four of her offspring to stand in front of the garden gate that she hadn't yet got round to painting (third year running). A picture of relative calm and serenity.

Back track two hours, 6.30am Mummy was awoken by two sons who had ignored her previous evening's request to not get up before 7am (when the alarm clock changes from blue to yellow). She decided to give them the benefit of the doubt and believe that they were just excited about their first day back at school. Mummy sent them downstairs and briefly thought about how fast the summer holidays had gone, but at the same time was kind of glad routine was returning as the previous week had just about finished her off when an end of holiday treat playing crazy golf finished off with two of her offspring wielding mini golf clubs as if they were fencing each other, chipping bits out of each other's shins/heads/kneecaps.

Usual morning routine ensued. Mummy managed to extricate her four-year-old from downstairs and got him ready in his new uniform upstairs and then disappeared to get herself ready. Upon emerging from the bathroom, Mummy discovered her four-year-old, now undressed, waiting for her outside, protesting that his uniform was too big. Mummy was now getting stressed that the previous aim of getting to school early was disappearing rapidly. Daddy got up and asked what was going on so Mummy asked Daddy to sort out his son and persuade him to wear uniform. Daddy re-dressed son (Daddy could sell sand to the Arabs).

Following a now rushed breakfast, all children ran upstairs to clean their teeth, Mummy requested that they try not to get toothpaste on their uniforms. They descended as Mummy went to clean her own teeth. Mummy asked them not to play outside as she hadn't had a chance to clean up dog poo yet.

Mummy came back down to find all four children playing outside. Coffee was grabbed, bags were grabbed, Mummy was just about to lock door when one of her sons came inside with his lunch bag and informed her that it smelt. Upon closer inspection, Mummy found out that it had been dropped in aforementioned, unpicked up dog poo. Son revealed that he and older sisters had been playing football with it (ignoring plethora of balls of all sizes and descriptions littering the back yard). Mummy stifled a frustrated scream as she disinfected the lunch-bag, loaded herself up with various bags and locked the door. Mummy ordered four children to stand by back gate and look happy. Maisie was asked to pull her skirt down a bit as the waistband was up under her armpits. Result was that Maisie has a sullen stroppy face pose for all but one of the photos. Mummy also spotted that eldest son had deposited toothpaste all down new school sweater, so dragged him to outside hose before resuming photograph pose.

Mummy was determined to not get a phone call from Miss Late Monitor this school year.

Everyone was in the car... and then it dawned on her...

Mummy quickly returned to the house to collect peacefully sleeping Baby Isla who ordinarily wakes up at the drop of a pin during the night but can happily sleep through the chaos of the pre-school morning antics. Mummy mentally told herself that she was not a bad mother, having forgot her fifth child in the house.

One car journey (and diversion later as Council had decided this week was a good week to start roadworks on two of the possible routes to school), Mummy waved goodbye to children.

"Off they go," thought Mummy, just in time as she was ready to sell them to the travelling circus by the time she waved them goodbye.

THE FIRST week of school went relatively well. Olly seemed to settle quickly in his all-day big boy school, after the initial morning of quivering lip. When Mummy collected him on his third day, the teacher was concerned that he appeared to be sent without any lunch. Mummy was most bewildered as she recalled definitely sending lunch in. Olly, it turned out later, had preferred the look of his teacher's lunch so ditched his and feigned "starving child". Mummy explained that this was not what we do.

On the first Friday Olly emerged from class clutching "Doti" aka the manhandled, grubby, germ-ridden, snot-marked, much-loved, stuffed dog who had to stay with him for the weekend and do lots of fun things with him and the rest of the family. "Yay," Mummy tried to look enthusiastic.

"First stop for Doti is the washing machine," thought Mummy. Having had Doti stay several times before with Olly's siblings when they were in Reception, Mummy had run out of ideas for things to do. Daddy offered to take Doti to work with him, as he had to work that weekend. Mummy subsequently spent that Sunday evening scrapping the photos Daddy had taken of Doti stuck in a coffin with only his squashed paw sticking out from under the lid and Doti subsequently downing a pint and replaced them with her own photos of Doti cuddled up in bed with Olly and going for a bike-ride with Opa. Mummy wondered whether it was school's way of checking on their parenting, perhaps they had installed a secret camera inside Doti? She would dearly love to chart Doti on a downward spiral but given that her four-year-old was going to have to explain it in class and not wanting to traumatise his classmates by having beloved Doti stuck in a coffin, she thought better of it.

GEORGE, THE pup, had simultaneously mastered the cutesie look and joined the Selective Listening Club that Mummy's offspring are all members of.

Daddy had gone to work at half past five the previous morning and he had been there fourteen hours. Mummy had slung George out for a wee at the same time and then let him back in but hadn't fed him. She went back to bed and slept through two alarms as, for once, Baby Isla had decided to gift her with more than four hours' sleep in a row, so George thought he would wake her up by eating her phone charger, which he thoroughly destroyed, leading to a second slinging out for him, during which time Mummy found the poop he had left her. He had, since then, been following her around everywhere, sitting on her feet when she stopped. He had intermittently disappeared to rescue shoes from the floor by the shoe cupboard (for some reason the shoes are never put IN the shoe cupboard). Daddy hadn't yet discovered that George had also chewed the top of his Doc Martins... Mummy decided not to break this news to him at the end of a long day, so George was still in Daddy's good books for the time being that evening.

George was besotted with Baby Isla. When Mummy lay her down to change her nappy, George lay down next to her. George was also firm friends with Olly and when Olly arrived home from school, they'd spend half an hour of the zoomies, zooming from room to room, before George took himself off to his bed for a rest. He had settled in just fine.

AFTER A particularly bad night with Baby Isla, Daddy had offered to take the children to school. On the way, Riley mentioned that they needed to take fruit and veg in with them. Daddy didn't question why but found a stray banana leftover from the other day that he had stuck in the side of his car door, he handed it over to Riley. When Daddy relayed this to Mummy, proud that he had sorted it, Mummy's brain cogs started turning and with horror she realised that she had forgotten it was the Harvest service at school that day and that the children were all asked to bring an item of food in, so alongside the beautiful baskets of fruit, vegetables, tins and gift-wrapped hamper-esque displays, Riley had handed in their meagre offering of a sweaty, battered banana. "Oh my days," thought a mortified Mummy. She resolved to take something with her when she went to collect her children that afternoon.

MUMMY ADDED a post to her social media feed, "If any of my neighbours happen to find ten bags for life stuffed inside each other in their back gardens, they have just been caught by the wind and blown out of the boot of my car."

It had been blowing a hooley when they had returned from school that afternoon. Incidentally, the main reason for the plethora of bags in Mummy's car-boot is that she turns up at the supermarket, determined to just pop in for one thing, so doesn't take a bag as she thinks by not taking a bag she will force herself to stick to her limit of just one item of shopping...but then when she reaches the checkout she finds that she has too many things to carry, so purchases another bag for life.

So, this particular morning, imagine Mummy's surprise when she opened the boot to put the pram in and found said Bags for life there before her eyes... It would appear one of her offspring had been helpful and managed to retrieve all but one of her shopping bags from the alleyway during the gale force wind that was blowing. Rather than relaying this useful information to Mummy, they had watched this crazed female being blown from pillar to post in the wind and the rain looking for said bags while the pram base rolled down the road in the wind. Riley had even commented on how cool her hair had looked being blown about in the wind. Meanwhile Isla was sitting screaming in the car because her elusive burp had decided to make an appearance and wake her up and Olly was sitting having a meltdown as he was scared the wind would blow him away. Her other three offspring sat watching Mummy who was trying not to lose the plot.

Some years ago, Mummy bought a clock for her offspring that turns yellow to indicate that they are allowed to get up. Mummy can count the number of times this has happened and her offspring have actually paid any attention to the clock on one finger.

Over the years, they had gone through the scenarios:

Mummy: "You are not allowed downstairs unless the clock is yellow."

Mummy: "You are not allowed to wake anyone up unless the clock is yellow... actually, if the clock is yellow, red, blue or pink you are NOT allowed to wake ANYONE up....do NOT wake up your sleeping brother/sister... IF the clock is yellow, be as quiet as a mouse and go downstairs."

Youngest, incredulous: "Do we have mice?"

Mummy hangs her head in despair.

You get the picture...

So, cue Monday morning. A groggy Mummy was woken up at 5.45am by two sons asking if they could go downstairs. The clock was not even close to being yellow.

Mummy, "What day is it?" like this was going to make a blind bit of difference. Sons can't remember what day it is because in their week it is either a day you go to school, or a day you stay at home and Monday to Sunday don't really have much meaning. "Is the clock yellow?" Mummy asks the rhetorical question.

"No" ... "Right, go back to bed until it's yellow, go to the toilet first though if you need it."

The new equation to the clock yellow business was George the pup. Since a recent incident involving him christening the bedroom carpet, he had been trained to sleep in the kitchen and not next to the bed. This was bliss as the puppy definitely has no concept of a yellow clock. For the first week this had worked. Now, when the eagle-eared puppy heard the slightest noise of awakeness upstairs, he would hurl his body at the kitchen door, which was ill-fitting and rattled.

Mummy dragged herself downstairs and put the puppy outside and then decides she had now given up on sleep, so began chores. Two sons arrived downstairs. Mummy had decided that she'd have to reinforce the clock with bribery.

On a Friday night, her sons were allowed to spend thirty pence on penny sweets at the kids' club their sisters attend which they were too young for yet. Mummy explained her plan to her boys: "Every day you get up before the clock is yellow, you will have five sweets deducted."

Oldest son does some quick maths... "But that means we get no sweets?"

"Correct," confirmed Mummy.

Oldest son: "But we can still have ice cream?"

Mummy gave up but marvelled at his bargaining skills.

"We're starting tomorrow," she declared.

Chapter 10

October

Mummy had been particularly sleep-deprived this week as Baby Isla had suddenly started waking up again for no rhyme or reason. Just as she thought that a routine had been cracked, something cropped up to upset the routine and Mummy felt like it started all over again.

Mummy's tether had very nearly run out. George, the pooch, had decided that destroying dog beds was his new favourite hobby, another dog bed had been destroyed the day before, leaving black bed-stuffing all over the kitchen floor.

Upon collecting children from school, Mummy informed them: "We'll just pop to the shop to get a new dog bed." All the kids were excited that said shop also sells sweeties so thought they may be able to do some twisting of Mummy's arm to buy sweeties too.

What Mummy had forgotten was that down the pet aisle, opposite the dog beds, were squeaky dog toys. Her two sons immediately made a beeline for annoying squeaky toys and proceeded to squeeze every single one of them. Olly discovered that you could sit on three of them at the same time and the wail they gave out was in stereo, making it sound like a wailing banshee was presiding over Aisle twelve.

Mummy found that wailing was getting right on her last nerve as she was faced with an array of dog beds with no price next to any of them.

Mummy turned to children and requested that this game now ended as she was having a hard job concentrating. At this point a jolly customer came down the aisle, laughing at the children who were having such fun.

Mummy has turned to continue her quest for most hardwearing, least destructible dog bed when a huge wail blasted her last nerve to smithereens. Without turning round, Mummy said in her sternest voice: "I SAID stop now with these toys."

Jolly customer apologetically confessed: "Sorry, that was me."

Mummy turned round and apologises, mortified, whilst her offspring fall about laughing at her. Thankfully, Mummy and jolly customer both saw the funny side of it.

Mummy found a suitable dog bed eventually and children received Sweetie Day sweets at home. George was very pleased with his new bed for the time being...

THE ADVANTAGE of having swimming lessons during the Autumnal months, is that at least the warmth of the spectator gallery is a welcome comfort. In the height of summer, not so much as on the hottest of summer days, Mummy feels like she has been pushed into a sauna, fully clothed.

Olly has well and truly settled into his swimming lessons. His first trip to the pool for lessons, he introduced himself to everyone in the leisure centre before going into class. Mummy was looking forward to this particular swimming lesson as Opa had kindly agreed to look after her other children during the lesson, so she dropped them all off at his and having deposited Olly at the pool-side door, bought herself a coffee from the new coffee machine and settled down to half watch Olly and half make some time to read something other than a book from school. The first time Mummy and Olly came, Olly had spotted Mummy halfway through the lesson and yelled: "Mummy, I love you", at the top of his voice, which totally melted Mummy's heart.

In the changing room after this particular lesson, a discussion took place with Olly,

Olly: "You know when you think things in your head you get rainbows?"

Mummy: "Rainbows?"

Olly: "Yes and they make you creative."

Mummy: "So what kind of things make you get rainbows in your head?"

Olly: "Looking at new houses."

Mummy nonplussed by this, wondering whether she has a property tycoon in the making.

Mummy: "Oh, Ok, what else?"

Olly: "Playing with my best friend and chocolate brownies and ice cream."

Mummy: "Oohh, yes, those are the best rainbow thoughts," she agrees as she also thinks how much she loves the very bones of this child of hers with his rainbow thoughts, thankful heart and willingness to just speak what is on his mind with no filter of needing it to make sense to anyone else.

Mummy and Olly went to collect his siblings from Opa's. Opa had recently introduced his grandchildren to "Les Miserables" which, much to Mummy's surprise, had completely captured their imaginations as Opa had explained the story. Now, whenever going to Opa's house, they always ask whether they can watch "Les Miserables" and Opa agrees. Mummy has never known her children quietly sit for more than ten minutes, never mind three hours, watching a film. Mummy has given up on cinema trips with her children for the time being after several unsuccessful attempts to go with them all, when, despite all going to the toilet before getting there, they appear to suffer from cinema-induced bladder retention issues and Mummy ends up spending more time in the cinema toilets with her individual children than in the actual film.

Mummy thanked Opa for his child-minding services and headed off home.

Later, post tea-time, Mummy was clearing up downstairs, four of her five kids were upstairs being quiet (which automatically raises her suspicion). The silence was broken by blood-curdling screams from Maisie. Mummy quickly assessed whether screams were indeed something to worry about or whether Maisie was being a drama queen. Riley then shouted that his sister had blood coming out of her nose. Mummy was upstairs in the blink of an eye. Truth was outed, Olly had been encouraged by Riley to re-enact the barricade scene from the French Revolution. In lieu of having a bayonet, Olly had jabbed a plastic sword up Maisie's nose... Crying all round as Mummy explained the ground rules for ensuring a peaceful and happy home in no uncertain terms. The historian in Mummy mused well at least their squabbling was set in a historical context. Her children... less "Les Mis" and more just miserable. "Bedtime it is," she declared... 'Bedtime it is."

AS OCTOBER was well underway, Mummy reflected on how she loves this season; the changes in the leaves and the stunning array of colours they produce, the fresh autumnal mornings and then gradually the crunch of leaves under her feet as the trees lose their leaves.

Mummy had grand plans prior to half term, in the absence of having to try and condense everything into the time between school drop-off and school pick-up; as well as it being an opportunity to spend time together with her children, she had planned to see a few friends, catch up on things she hadn't caught up on recently like trying out a few baking/craft projects, reading a book or two that don't involve the antics of Biff, Chip and Kipper, discovering some new walks and generally relaxing.

The week before half term, Daddy received an urgent phone call from a business contact who was demanding, so he relays to Mummy, that he join them on an all-expenses paid business golf trip in a nice hotel an hour away as someone has pulled out. Daddy felt he couldn't let them down. Mummy thought she'd happily help them out of their predicament and Daddy could stay home with five kids for forty-eight hours alone (Mummy has only ever had one golf lesson and accidentally chipped a hole in one and for some reason Daddy has never encouraged her to try any more lessons).

So, seven days into half term and twenty-six hours into Daddy being on his urgent business trip, the total sum of adult books read was zero, total bakes done was four, total number of loads of washing done was that many, Mummy wondered whether she had extra guests in the house that someone had failed to inform her of.

Mummy and the kids had also taken Nana for a morning out during which time Nana had surveyed the latest styles of stripy socks being modelled in M&S and declared that "this odd sock fashion has obviously come over from America" which has left Mummy befuddled and mildly amused that Nana has thrown the odd sock fashion into Nana's Room 101 along with all things foreign and any food that hasn't been cooked to within an inch of its life.

Mummy also discovered that a morning given over to a four-mile hike with the promise of a hot chocolate at the end of it equals an afternoon of relative peace and quiet as the kids are too tired to argue and less likely to kill each other. Baby Isla was quite content, being strapped to Mummy's back and bobbing up and down as she slept and Mummy walked.

One such walk, done with her friend, Cara and her children, on a cold, frosty day, resulted in an afternoon tea at one of Mummy and Cara's favourite tearooms. Mummy had forgotten that this is a tearoom for ladies who lunch, or yummy mummies still in the glow of babies, designer slings and Cath Kidston change bags. Mummy lost the glow a number of children ago.

As Mummy, Cara and six rag-tag, muddy, just-walked-four-miles bunch of kids walk in like they're emerging from an adventure with Bear Grylls, it is noted that they are a stark contrast to the local mummy's lunch group who are sporting their pumpkin-costumed-chubby babies at the nearby table. After six rag-tag kids had been given half a month's quota of sugar in the form of milkshake and cake (and after Mummy had retrieved Riley off the top of the wobbling seat cushions that he had stacked as high as possible in an effort to win the who-can-stay-on-top-the-longest competition), Mummy and Cara ordered children to play outside in the hitherto quiet tearoom garden, enabling them to pretend that those rowdy children, who were currently throwing ice discs at each other from the frozen water in the dog water bowl, belonged to someone else for a blissful ten minutes. From the tearoom French doors they could be seen and not heard which gave the antics of the children outside a similar effect to a Silent Movie. As one child hurtled towards the French door window, which had also doubled up as base for the game of tag that was now underway, the two ladies sat in front of the window look rather alarmed and so Mummy and Cara went to reclaim their kids.

Once home; children fed, watered, showered and put to bed, Mummy decided to start Shabby Chicifying a recently acquired piece of furniture. Mummy thinks it'll only need one coat, at the most two.

Four coats of paint later; accompanied by late-night radio, copious amounts of tea and a cat and a puppy who are all very interested in what Mummy was up to and insistent on trying to jump onto freshly-painted furniture, only breaking to read the text from her husband telling her what a first-class three-course meal he had just enjoyed, Mummy was looking more shabby than chic and decided to call it a day and head for bed.

No sooner had her head hit the pillow she awoke to a child standing over her, his face inches from hers and she momentarily thought she had awoken in some Japanese horror film, but then refocused and realised it was Olly. Following a toilet trip, he decided to not go back to his own bed, but to make the most of Daddy's side of the bed being unoccupied. Mummy was so dog-tired she agreed and consequently spent the rest of the night attempting to sleep with a rather affectionate heat-seeking missile, who decided to rise and shine at 6am.

Despite it being early, Mummy couldn't help treasuring the moment as this little one wrapped his arms around her neck, planted a big kiss on her cheek and then unburdened his four-year-old soul. Mummy was enjoying not having to rush.

Upon his return, Daddy suggested a weekend trip to Opa's caravan to end half-term and Mummy agreed.

MUMMY MADE a mental note; "Whilst on a weekend break at the caravan and it is pitch black and slinging it down outside, if you find you are short of milk, do not decide to nip out and get some more."

One Mummy failed to see the mud bath awaiting her at the bottom of the steps, flew and landed flat on her back... got up and decided to press on in her quest to get milk... one driver's seat now very muddy... Arrived at the shop and assessed the damage under lights to find that the only pair of jeans she had brought with her are absolutely laden with mud... so bought milk and then realised that a trip to the 24-hour supermarket was going to have to take place to buy some non-muddy replacement jeans. She arrived at the supermarket looking like she was some long-lost explorer emerging from the depths of the jungle, bedraggled and bottom notably soggy and saggy. Got to the jeans rail and was accosted by all manner of jean types... boot cut, slim cut, skinny, super skinny, mid rise, high rise... what happened to plain old jeans? Finally found a pair that weren't going to make her look ridiculous and returned to the caravan, avoiding the mud bath at the entrance, to her husband who looked up from his book, surprised at the length of time it had taken to get a pint of milk.

3AM MUMMY had designated Tied-Up-Outside-to-the Caravan-Steps as the makeshift "in the doghouse" as George sat there looking at her, forlorn.

A little dog means that he can join in with the rest of the family and accompany them on their relaxing weekends at the caravan. Former life with one large dog meant Mummy had to arrange dog care because there was no way they would all fit in the caravan with four growing children as well as the large dog.

Daddy had looked at Mummy on night one at the caravan and remarked: "I can't believe how much easier it is to have him along with us."

Daytime was fine whilst dry, but as the thunderstorm and torrential rain set in, George had decided he was not too keen on going out to do his business, so despite Mummy standing out there with him in the piddling rain at various points throughout the evening, he decided to refrain.

Cue 3am: All were fast asleep. Mummy was woken by Olly leaning over her. Mummy avoided headbutting her son and asked what was wrong.

"George has pooed under Nell's bed," relayed Olly.

Mummy looked; George was snoring his little head off enjoying his doggy dream in the corner of the bedroom. Mummy hauled herself out of bed to go and investigate, creeping past Isla sleeping peacefully in her cot.

Mummy discovered all four children wide awake with the odour of George's parcel permeating their room.

Mummy grabbed the sleeping dog, trundled down the steps onto the wet grass and rudely dumped him down on the temporary doggy naughty step, leaving him to give the neighbouring caravan competition to rival their previous night's drunken rendition of John Denver's "Take

Me Home Country Roads" that went on long into the night.

Mummy reappeared, poo bags, disinfectant, torch and scrubbing equipment at the ready and found that it wasn't that easy to squish herself sideways through the gap between beds (approximately a thirty cm gap) quietly.

As she surveyed the task ahead in the furthest corner under the bed, Mummy did wonder how the dog managed to even get under there, let alone squat. Mummy shuffled on her tummy under the bed like a rather clumsy tortoise and dealt with the offending parcel whilst Olly decided now was the time to get out of bed to go to the loo as he stood on the only part of Mummy's body that wasn't squished under the bed. Mummy let off some threatening whispers but, unsurprisingly, as most of Mummy was flat on her face under the bed, her orders and threats weren't carrying quite the same disciplinary weight that they normally did. Mummy shuffled backwards, turned sideways and attempted to pull herself sideways through the impossibly small gap between the beds as gracefully as a hippopotamus trying to get out of a small dog kennel.

Successful, out into the damp grass in bare feet Mummy trundled, whispering murderous threats at the pup who shut up.

Pup was deposited back inside, Mummy told very wide-awake children to go back to sleep and Mummy took herself back to bed, where He who had declared it so much easier at the caravan with a small dog lay snoring quietly, oblivious to the whole debacle.

Mummy put her cold, damp feet on her husband. "Humpph," she said as she closed her eyes.

Chapter 11
November

After seventeen years of marriage and a month or so of lower back pain, Mummy and Daddy realised that their mattress was probably the issue and had bitten the bullet and the previous month gone out to buy a new one. Talk about stressful, the children thought that they had been taken to a trampoline park and had bounced from one bed to another whilst Mummy and Daddy were testing mattresses at the other end of the store. When Mummy caught Nell about to do one of her handsprings using the bed like a springboard, a decision on the mattress had been made and Daddy had been left to sort out paying for it whilst Mummy herded her four bigger children and a pram out of the store to the car before they ended up having to pay for umpteen broken beds.

Three weeks later the new mattress was delivered. Mummy had to stop George attempting to hump the delivery man's leg on his way in.

That evening, Daddy and Mummy manoeuvred the new mattress upstairs with much effing, jeffing and attempting not to knock small humans flying down the stairs all of whom had abandoned watching cartoons as they were very inquisitive and wanting to "help". Removing the old mattress was easier in comparison and it was deposited outside, along with one of the children's mattresses which had also seen better days.

That evening, the heavens opened and it lashed it down all evening. Mummy phoned the Council the next day to arrange for a "bulky items" collection. The Council lady informed Mummy that if the mattresses were to be left outside, they should be covered up, as it would just be one Council employee turning up in a few days' time in his van to collect said mattresses and if they were too wet, they would be too heavy and he wouldn't take them. Mummy was absorbing this information whilst looking at the already soaking wet mattresses through her kitchen window. She had retrieved the plastic wrapping from the bin and covered the sopping wet mattresses up.

Five days later, Mummy had done battle with this king-size mattress each day as it had been insistent that it wasn't going to stand on its side. George had also decided that the mattress was a deadly sworn enemy that he must protect his household from, leading him to bark incessantly each time he was put out in the garden.

Sunday morning had dawned, there was an amber weather warning in place and gale force winds had sent the plastic wrapping flying. As Mummy retrieved the wrapping from the tree in sixty-mile-an-hour winds, dressed in her dressing gown and slippers, she decided she was fed up of waiting for the Council, especially as Riley's birthday was coming up and she had opted to host the birthday party at home. She didn't want a mattress lying around.

After Church, as she retrieved the plastic wrapping from the alleyway (again), Mummy decided to try and load mattresses into the back of her car, along with all manner of tat that needed to be taken to the local recycling centre, on her own (Daddy was out for the day and the kids had gone for lunch to Nana's so that Mummy could get the party preparations sorted).

"How hard can it be?" said Mummy to herself.

Very hard, that's how hard.

As five feet two and a half inches, Mummy heaved a king-size sodden mattress (it had rained for the past five days) across the yard in high winds to the awaiting empty boot of her car, the thought did cross her mind that she may have underestimated the wind speed slightly. She managed to semi fold the mattress and heave it halfway into the boot, then went round to the other side of the car and got in to pull it further in, just as neighbour Janice's latest gentleman friend walked down the alleyway (which her car was blocking). He was presented with Mummy's rear end poking between the front seats as she heave-hoed the mattress as far as possible into the car. Not her best angle, admittedly.

Satisfied with her efforts, Mummy returned to the garden to get the single mattress, which was unexpectedly drier and considerably lighter than the king-size one. The wind caught the mattress and Mummy took off with the mattress towards the car. She quickly realised that the only way of stopping it taking off like a magic carpet was to throw herself unceremoniously on top of it to stop it in its tracks.

Neighbour Geoff who had been watching through his blinds, opened his window and shouted out to Mummy, "Need any help?". Geoff was not a stranger to Mummy's escapades. He is an elderly gentleman who had lost his wife a few years ago, round about the same time that Mummy had lost her Mum. Mummy and Geoff had struck up an unlikely friendship over the years, walking their dogs together, Mummy kept Geoff plied with any extra cookies, cakes and bakes she was in the habit of making. She was very thankful that Geoff DID keep an eye out as he had helped her out of tricky situations in the past, most recently early last summer (pre-pregnancy) when Mummy had been making the most of the kids still being at school and decided to spend a day gardening. There were a lot of weeds, so she had been trying to get ultimate usage out of her green gardening bin, negating the need for a trip to the tip, by flattening it down. Ordinarily, she'd get one of the kids to don their wellies and get them jumping up and down in the bin, but as she was home alone, she had decided to do it herself. She had got in the bin somehow, squished it all down and then she couldn't get out and had found herself to be completely and utterly stuck. Thankfully, Geoff had been in his garden and heard her calls for help. Geoff had come to the rescue and had to carefully tip the green bin over so Mummy could crawl out, like an oversized, very embarrassed, caterpillar. It had taken Mummy a while to look him in the eye after that. She hadn't even told her husband and, full credit to him, Geoff had kept that little secret to himself.

She assured Geoff that she was OK, albeit rather unconvincingly as she was flat on her face, splayed on a mattress in the garden in the middle of November. Eventually, with both mattresses firmly in the car, Mummy gingerly took a very slow drive to the local tip with her boot open and the car beeping warning alerts all the way to alert her to the fact that the boot was open.

Mummy is on first name terms with all the local recycling centre staff as she is a regular depositer of junk there.

Thankfully, they are also very helpful and sort all her rubbish for her.

Mummy returned home; rubbish free, dishevelled and windswept to have a much-needed cup of tea.

"AND IT'S ok to leave him here for the party?" asked Freddy's Dad. Freddy is Riley's best bud. Freddy is a cheeky, red-headed, freckled Babyface.

"Yes, sure," said Mummy, innocently and unsuspecting. "Pick him up in two hours."

She should have known when Freddy's Dad virtually turned around and sprinted off to the awaiting car (that, incidentally, still had the engine running and Freddy's Mum with her foot at-the-ready on the accelerator). Come to think of it, the question "and it's okay to leave him here?" was asked with a certain amount of incredulity. So... Babyface, rather like the hulk on his T-shirt, turned into The Baby-faced Assassin the minute the door shut. He proceeded to whirl through the house like the hurricane that was blowing outside, leaving no Lego box unturned, no dressing-up box unemptied. He had even managed to find the long-lost armband we had given up looking for last year; attempting to inflate it up with his baby-faced painted hulk mouth, not getting very far and then offering up the armband to Daddy to inflate. Daddy, completely oblivious to the amount of hulk slobber that had been generously deposited around valve, had happily obliged.

Little did Babyface. know that this Mummy, as well as having five little kids of her own, also had eighteen years' experience of dealing with hard-core ex-offenders under her belt. Babyface had met his match. He thought he'd opt out of the party games, Mummy used the tone no one argues with, quiet but firm, so Babyface consented to being in the same room as everyone else but refused to partake in the festivities until he realised sweeties were the prize and then he shook his booty as if his life depended on it.

Party food time was more akin to feeding time at the zoo with Babyface sampling each piece of food and then returning it to the platter if he didn't like it, Mummy had to explain to Babyface that Baby Isla was not allowed to try cocktail sausages dipped in chocolate fondue...

Daddy did a sterling job of post party-tea Stick the Tail on the donkey game and then all the boys ended up having a Nerf-gun shoot out.

Finally, parents of Baby-Faced Assassin, having had two hours' free childcare, turned up at the appointed time looking refreshed and invigorated. Mummy and Daddy returned Babyface back to his rightful owners. They may look refreshed now, but they were now going to have to endure the aftermath of two hours of their Baby-Faced Assassin being stoked up with Haribos, chocolate and all kinds of E numbers. He was a ticking timebomb...

BABY ISLA was already five months old. Mummy and Daddy had decided to reclaim their bedroom and move her into her own. Mummy didn't understand how she could sleep through all manner of white noise or, in fact, the general hullabaloo during the day and yet as soon as it was the dead of night, a mere pin drop would wake her, so Daddy's snoring was not conducive to her sleeping. Daddy says Mummy snores. Mummy begs to differ, she fails to see how Daddy, who had managed to sleep through nine years of the nocturnal shenanigans of his offspring, could now claim that her snoring kept him up... nope, she didn't snore.

So, Mummy had started as she meant to go on, she fed Isla, sang to her and placed her in her cot. Isla was happy as long as Mummy was making contact with her. Mummy had tried gradually withdrawing her hand with the care that you would need to diffuse a ticking time bomb. No sooner was her hand out of the way, Isla's eyes sprang open and she was wide awake again. This had now been going on for a few nights, turning into a back-and-forth ritual until Mummy had finally discovered that one of the cuddly toys in Isla's cot, if touching her with a certain pressure, tricked her into thinking that it was still Mummy's hand on her. Now that that problem was solved, Mummy had to get out of her room without standing on any squeaky floorboards. Mummy was somewhat of an expert when it came to squeaky floorboards, a skill perfected in her late teenaged years when she still lived in her parental home. She would arrive home late and embark on a Krypton Factor-like mini assault course across the hall landing to get into her room without her Mum and Dad finding out. The times she had tip-toed on one particular board, flat left foot at a right angle on the next, a slight jump 30cms to the left... So, she had put her plan into action and established just how much pressure each floorboard could withstand. That night, just as she had successfully managed to extricate herself from Isla's room with the level of stealth that would impress a cat burglar, Daddy had pounded up the stairs like a herd of elephants, yawning loudly and woken Isla up. Mummy gave him the bells of Shannon before returning to her Krypton Factor pursuits with her youngest.

A NUMBER of months ago, at the start of the new school year, Nell begged Mummy and Daddy to let her take up the clarinet as there was an offer of lessons in school. Daddy had encouraged Nell in this choice as he imagined Gershwin ringing through the house.

Nell had been so excited at breakfast today as it was the day that she was allowed to bring her instrument home. Up until now they had had to borrow school instruments.

Eight hours later, after school. Gershwin... it was not. Mummy and Daddy had been listening to Nell's practice for twenty minutes and it sounded more like a goose in the throes of a long, drawn-out death. George had decided it was offensive to his ears and begun to howl along, which, in turn, had set Isla off crying, adding to the cacophony that was music practice. "Here's hoping she improves quickly," Mummy thought, as she was not sure her nerves could handle this for very long. "I will be burying that clarinet in a coffin along with my soul if that carries on much longer," remarked Daddy.

MUMMY WAS sat at quarter to midnight, having only just finished ironing. Mummy hates ironing with a passion that surprises her. Ironing had been delayed as it had taken longer than usual to put the shopping away. She had been interrupted by Maisie shouting down from upstairs that all the towels in the airing cupboard were soaking wet. Upon investigation there was a slow drip from the boiler above the towels which had led to them being sodden... so, an early evening visit from a plumber friend, with his three kids in tow, ensued, much to the delight of her own kids who were gleeful that their school friends had come over and bedtime was temporarily delayed so they could terrorise each other, the cat and the dog.

So, Mummy had decided to actually sit down for five minutes, even though it was late and even though she was tired, to have a late-night hot chocolate and catch up with herself. It was her Mum's favourite hot chocolate. It got her to thinking about her Mum. It was only five years ago that she had said a final goodbye to Mum. After a short battle with Motor Neurone Disease, she had passed away unexpectedly.

Just six months earlier, Mummy had been to visit her parents in their German home. They lived there at the time. These were her favourite times; all the kids asleep in bed, her Dad asleep and she would sit in their small kitchen late at night and finally get a chance to just chat with her Mum; they'd have a hot chocolate and share their hearts. Some nights they'd listen to a late-night audio book together.

"My dear Mum, she was with me at my first breath, I was with her at her last."

Grief is such an untamed ocean, some days calm, other days stormy. She had felt battered by the storm those past few days, her heart felt raw and she was just physically exhausted from the emotional upset of an anniversary where reality caught her and that cold realisation gripped her raw heart as she realised she wouldn't see Mum again in this life. How much she would have loved to have seen the children growing, to meet Isla, to have been amidst the hustle and bustle that was every day. All of this missed and yet she is so much a part of it all as Mummy recognises traits of Mum running through herself and her children.

It was also just this season of the run-up to Christmas. It always makes her think of Mum. She would always bake an enormous Christmas cake, weeks in advance (that would probably feed the five thousand and then some). It would take seven hours to bake. One year she forgot to put glycerin in the icing and you literally had to take a sledgehammer to it to open it up. Mum would split the cake into quarters and give Mummy and her siblings a quarter each to eat in their respective homes. It would normally tide them over until Easter. One year, when Charlie had been a pup, Mummy arrived home one day to find that Charlie had jumped up and retrieved the foil wrapped quarter off the kitchen side and devoured the lot. It made for one sick puppy. And then there was the year Mum made an alcoholic fruit punch and misread the measurements. Everyone ended up very overcome with refreshment.

"Oh Mum, what I would give to just have one of our late-night chats. In this season coming up, memories of you invade my thoughts. Ahh, Mum. Miss you, I do...Hiraeth," thought Mummy.

IT WAS the last day of November. The elves were due to make a come-back.

Mummy has spent her morning trying to retrieve them from the Christmas box which in her wisdom she had put right at the bottom of the only storage cupboard in the house with a zillion things piled on top which fell out on her as she opened the cupboard. This is the cupboard where all the rammel that is lying around the hallway gets slung if there are visitors coming. As Mummy piled it all back in, she made a mental note of everything she didn't use that she really needed to take along to the charity shop at some point.

The first year that the elves appeared it was a novelty and Mummy primarily saw Chippy the elf not as Santa's little helper, but more there to help her achieve whatever desired outcome she had so far not secured through traditional parenting methods. Mummy was now kicking herself as rather than phasing the elves out, Chippy had been joined by Ernie and at one stage Elsie (until the dog chewed her head off... that was a debacle Mummy would rather not remember... four inconsolable children one very early morning).

The authenticity of Chippy was momentarily called into question when Maisie read the label on his bottom and asked: "Why is he made in China?". That was quickly skirted over and, low and behold, Chippy's label mysteriously disappeared. Unfortunately, Mummy's girls were now older and wiser and the elves are no longer able to be used as a bargaining tool.

Olly spent all of the previous day extremely excited, hacking an old shoebox to bits to make it into an elf house, writing notes and wrapping Oxo Cube boxes filled with marshmallows as presents. This involved Mummy all along the way and Mummy, sporting a chest cold, had zero energy or enthusiasm to muster up for anything elf related. Olly was now about to spend a month believing himself to be a fellow elf, putting paid to any of Mummy's attempts to instil the real meaning behind Christmas. Olly and his siblings had been poring over the toy shop catalogue since it arrived in early October and Mummy has had to prepare her children for the fact that simply circling an item in the catalogue did not necessarily guarantee delivery of that item.

At 10pm Daddy woke Mummy up from her snooze in front of the telly and told her to go to bed and Mummy realised she still had to sort out the elf activity for the night before bed. Mummy quickly scanned the internet for some bright ideas and landed on one that looked easy enough to engineer.

Chapter 12
December

December 1st. Early.

Mummy and Daddy were awoken by the delighted guffaws of youngest son who had discovered Chippy and Ernie elves had snuck in through the letterbox overnight and one of them had got stuck. "Ahh, Christmas is soon going to be here," thought Mummy. Even Daddy (who normally relishes a lie-in and is like a bear with a sore head if he gets woken up too early on a day off) lay there laughing at the giggles from downstairs. Chippy and Ernie joined in with all the activities of the day.

December 2nd. Earlier than early.

It was still dark and sons crept in to ask Mummy whether they could go downstairs to see what the elves had got up to in the night. Mummy said no as the clock was most definitely not yellow yet. Riley and Olly appeared to both be colour blind as whatever the colour of the clock, they still came in and woke Mummy up asking if they could go downstairs. After six of these conversations and for an easy life, Mummy relented and ordered boys downstairs.

December 3rd. 5.45am

"Have you actually even been to bed?" asked Mummy to her two sons, at the ready, stood like two pyjama-clad soldiers at Mummy's side of the bed.

By the end of day three, elves had been blamed for wet towels on the floor in the bathroom, eating the cat food, the almighty mess in the boys' bedroom, not putting the dirty dishes away. Savvy children. Frazzled Mummy had again resorted to using threat, "if you don't... (choose whichever task you desire child to do immediately) ... then those elves are going back to the North Pole and staying there forever...

Upon laying her tired, sorry body in bed that night, Mummy had the realisation just before she was about to fall asleep that despite the fact she had spent most of the day sorting out the chaos that the elves had apparently left in their wake, somehow she had forgotten to put them in their nightly positions of whatever naughtiness they were up to now. Mummy proceeded to haul her body out of bed to the kitchen, where George was asleep; she rooted around and found string, creating a zip line effect from dining room light to candle holder on the wall. Elves were carefully placed, mid-air from the zip line. Previously sleeping pup was now awake, surveying with one beady eye, as his dishevelled owner was balancing on the dining room table trying not to pull the dining room light down in her efforts. Mummy returned to bed.

December 4th. Stupid o'clock.

George was throwing himself at the dining room door, barking and going berserk as he had decided Chippy and Ernie were intruders as he had spotted them suspended from the "zip wire" across the dining room.

Dog woke up entire household (apart from Daddy).

Mummy took elves down, knocking the candle holder off the wall in the process, further adding to the noise as this wrought iron construction hit the floor.

Nell grumpily told her that she wished the elves hadn't come as now her younger brothers got up even earlier than they did already. Mummy was under the table retrieving candle holder and trying to find the missing candle which she realised George had in his mouth. She was rueing the day she had brought these blasted elves into the house. The realisation had hit her that she had at least five more years of this elf business. What had she done...? She wondered whether the elves could chance upon an untimely end in the next two years before Baby Isla is old enough to realise what was going on, or was Mummy destined to spend another 12 years scouring Pinterest for elf ideas?

December 5th.

When Mummy arrived downstairs for breakfast this morning, she found that Nell had taken it upon herself to create a naughty and good list for her siblings and had appointed herself both arbiter and judge, deciding which category their behaviour fell into in the run up to Christmas. She had also created a "Rules of the house" – the rules mainly consisted of not doing things that her little brothers do that annoy her. One of her siblings had obviously got downstairs before Mummy and neatly ripped both pieces of paper in half. Mummy thought "welcome to Leadership, Nell, welcome to leadership that is what you call feedback".

AHH... THE first of two Christmas shows Mummy and Daddy were attending this week; Reception and Year one. Unfortunately Mummy and Daddy were sat next to a small child (not one of theirs) who had filled its nappy so there was a rather unpleasant aroma to contend with. They had managed to farm out the remainder of their children to Nana while they attended. They went to the back of the school hall to buy a mince pie (which is where the parents were asked to provide mince pies and donate them to the school, which they obediently did, only to then buy them back at an increased price at the Christmas Concert). School made 100 per cent profit. "Not a bad gig they've got going on here," remarked Daddy when he worked it out.

As they settled into their seats, Daddy quietly muttered under his breath, "Well, here begins an hour of our lives we'll never get back". Mummy shushed him.

Riley was looking uncomfortably warm in his sheep outfit, the Star had been whisked off the stage to the loo, there were only two wise men as apparently the third one was off sick and Freddy (aka BabyFace) had gone beyond bored and was now trying to see how tight he could pull his antler headdress round his neck. Come to think of it, Mummy was not sure she remembered there being any reindeer in Bethlehem.

As the show proceeded, one of the angels stumbled from her perch on top of the blocks at the back of the stage which Daddy thought was hilarious... a fallen angel... Mummy shushed him. One of the shepherds told the wise men to go away (it turned out it was his brother) and whilst Mary and Joseph were unsuccessfully searching for a room, Baby Jesus (a plastic doll) made an untimely appearance falling out from under the dress that Mary was wearing. "If only it were that easy," muttered Mummy to Daddy. Daddy muffled a snigger.

Joseph then grabbed Baby Jesus and stuffed him back under Mary's dress at which point Mummy and Daddy were giggling like a pair of kids and Mrs Owen, one of the Heads of Infants gave them a threatening stare.

They only had another three of these shows to look forward to.

MAISIE HAD been betwixt and between what she wanted for Christmas. Mummy was trying to focus the kids on narrowing it down to something you want, something you need, something to wear, something to read and something to do in order to keep things under control.

Mummy went up to tuck Maisie into bed when she got home. Maisie whispered to her,

"I know what I would like for Christmas, Mummy."

Mummy (fully expected yet another suggestion of a pay-through-the-nose-for-a piece-of-tat-toy); "What, love?"

"A new baby brother," said Maisie. "Ahh... that isn't going to happen, love," says Mummy thinking to herself that there was probably more chance of her getting that horse she had been asking for... fat chance and no chance of either.

AS WELL as the usual bustle of getting ready for Christmas, Mummy and Daddy also managed the perfect timing of Nell being born in the three weeks leading up to Christmas. So, as well as the four Christmas shows they have had to attend, Mummy had also planned another child's birthday party, although this one was a far more civilised affair than Riley's with a handful of friends, a few games, food and a movie.

Every year, Daddy and Mummy have very different run-ups to Christmas when it comes to organising things in the home.

Daddy basically leaves everything until Christmas week and then pops out one afternoon and in the space of an hour and a half, completes his Christmas shopping, which is basically presents for his wife.

Mummy starts organising and planning in October and aims to have all presents bought by the beginning of December so that she can actually take time in December to immerse her soul in what Christmas is really all about for her and not the materialistic debacle it has been made into. That said, school has requirements and children have requirements, so a balance is struck.

She had remembered Christmas Jumper day, bought all but a few of the presents and was mid-way through wrapping. She had been kick-started into wrapping when Maisie just happened to request a present that Mummy had already bought and stashed upstairs for Nell. Mummy wasn't convinced that Maisie hadn't been on the hunt for presents. Daddy enquired as to whether Mummy had begun present shopping the other evening and was astonished when Mummy confirmed she had already finished most of it.

She dragged herself along to the school Christmas Fayre where she "oohed and aahed" over the Christmas cards and craft that her children had made during school (which she could probably have done at home if truth be told). Unfortunately, these craft items were held to ransom until Mummy handed over a wadge of cash which apparently was to go towards raising money for the school (and not the staff night out). Nell was over the moon to win the raffle and be the proud owner of a new alarm clock. Mummy thought, "If there is any house that doesn't require an alarm clock, it's ours given that sleep deprivation levels are at the torturous end of the spectrum."

AND SUDDENLY the reason her daughter had emerged from her school Christmas Fayre with the odd prize of a cheap plastic blue alarm clock became abundantly clear as Mummy at 2.56am was awoken from her slumber and drawn unwittingly into some kind of challenge game show as she attempted to find beeping alarm clock without breaking her neck before said alarm clock woke any of her sleeping children. Mummy pounced on offending article, having groggily stumbled through two of three bedrooms, only to find that it was set for 7.00am, so no reason for 2.56am beep and all five children and their Daddy had managed to sleep through their mother's nocturnal challenge show bumblings. Mummy on the other hand, was now wide awake.

IN ADDITION to Christmas and birthdays, this year marked the 50th Wedding Anniversary of one of Mummy's Aunts and Uncles, so a family event had been planned, where Aunts, Uncles, Opa, Sisters, Brothers, Cousins and Second Cousins would all be in attendance. Mummy LOVES these events, a chance to see everyone and make some treasured memories. Daddy doesn't.

Daddy had been like a bear with a sore head at the thought of this impending family get-together, so was somewhat gleeful when the weather forecast heralded Storm Deidre; snow, ice, freezing rain and treacherous conditions.

The family get-together was a six-hour drive away. Daddy was insistent that they weren't driving there in this weather. A compromise was agreed and Mummy decided last minute to go by train with her crew. Daddy offered to stay at home and look after the dog and cat (who would ordinarily go days without being fed if it weren't for Mummy).

Two hours into the train journey, Mummy wondered why she hadn't thought of this earlier... children were happy colouring, reading, playing Lego Batman. Mummy decided to sit down with her book after purchasing a coffee, a bag of popcorn and a chocolate bar for the kids to share, for which she was charged the equivalent of an all-expenses paid trip to Mauritius.

Three hours in, having had four trips to the train toilet, which rather surprisingly started talking to you once you locked the door, briefly leading you to wonder whether there was a hidden camera somewhere in the vicinity and whether this was being streamed live throughout the carriage. Her crew were getting fractious.

Mummy inflicted "The Look" on Olly, who was stuck with his face peeking between the seats trying to get the attention of the balding gentleman further down the carriage by shouting: "Hey, Mr Bald Man". Mummy was not impressed. He desisted and started asking whether, instead, he could take his clothes off and put on his Captain America costume which he had somehow managed to smuggle into his bag. Mummy tried to explain that "that isn't necessarily a good idea, how about waiting until we get there?"

A few hours later, Mummy, four children and Captain America were navigating the London Underground. Mummy had promised children a McDonald's and then failed to find one which had led Captain America to have a meltdown as Mummy chivvied them through the throngs of Christmas shoppers to the final train of the day, doing a continual headcount as she went to make sure they were all accounted for.

They reached their destination two hours later with only one more small incident involving youngest son stroking feathery hat of lady sitting in front of him.

As kids were put to bed, Mummy sank into the sofa with a Merlot and relaxed into catching up with two of her cousins. They talked long into the night. Thankfully, this weekend Mummy could actually rest as all her kids played with their cousins and one baby was passed round adoring family. Also, elves had decided to remain at home with Daddy.

IT WAS Christmas Eve and mummy was trying to be really organised, peeling veg ready for the following day. Isla was bouncing along in her bouncer to the music on the radio. Mummy suddenly thought it was unusually quiet in the rest of the house. She went upstairs to find out what her children were up to as quietness, unless they were asleep, usually signalled mischief of some description.

Upon entering the boys' bedroom, she found a full-scale re-organisation of furniture going on, spearheaded by Nell. For once her siblings were doing as they were instructed.

"Umm, hey folks," Mummy announced her entrance. The children stopped what they were doing, "Can I just ask what is going on?". They live in an old house and there is a fireplace in every room, none of them used.

"Oh, we wanted it to be clear for Father Christmas because downstairs is blocked up," Nell explained, "We thought he could come down this chimney upstairs and walk downstairs if you leave the baby gates open."

Mummy managed to reassure them that he has his ways of getting into houses without functioning chimneys so no need for movement of furniture. She suggested that they settle down and watch a film. Unanimously they all agreed they wanted to watch "Home Alone", so Mummy sorted out popcorn and film for an hour or two. She aimed to get them to bed on time tonight as she still had a list of things to do. They had invited Opa, Nana and Geoff for lunch the following day. There was the ever-present threat of Daddy being called out to work on Christmas Day which could totally put the kibosh on plans.

Before bed, Mummy had to have a word with Riley and explain that it was not acceptable to refer to your sisters as "filthy animals". Unsurprisingly, they were both indignant. Mummy thought perhaps Home Alone might not have been the best choice for an impressionable young boy.

MUMMY WAS still in the kitchen sorting out Christmas day food, when Olly came downstairs in tears,

"What's the matter sweetheart?" asked Mummy. Olly, between sniffs... "My... my... Stocking has gone... has Farmer Christmas been and taken it and not filled it?"

Mummy actually had the stockings in the corner of the kitchen in a bag ready to fill, she had removed them from the ends of beds just half an hour after she thought everyone had fallen asleep. She made a mental note to not to do THAT again.

Mummy assured him Father Christmas had not been and she had removed stocking to... "Darn it... Yes... Darn it... there was a small hole in it..."

She took Olly back up to bed and repositioned the stocking. This could be a long night.

11:30pm – The house was quiet. Daddy had already gone to bed. Everything was ready. Mummy sat down in the kitchen and took a breath, talked to her Maker and quietened her soul. Thankful.

Christmas Day Evening.

Mummy sat down next to Daddy for a late-night buffet of crackers and cheese another Christmas Day over. All in all a success as she thought about the day. Thankfully, the kids didn't wake up much earlier than normal. There were squeals of delight at all the presents. Between them, Daddy and Mummy spent a good fifteen minutes trying to open up the packaging that the toys were in, wires, screws and rubber bands securing them all. The cat came and sat in one of the boxes watching the chaos while George took off with the wrapping paper.

They all went to Church, the Christmas Day service is always a relaxed affair, mainly children bringing up their presents to show everyone. As the pastor talked about memorable Christmas, he opened it up for congregation participation, "does anyone have a Christmas that stands out?"

Harry put his hand up. Harry is an extremely suave, well-dressed eighty-five-year-old gentleman. The way he speaks reminds Mummy of one of these gentlemen who lounge about in day-dressing-gowns puffing on a cigarette in a holder. Harry has just started seeing Elsie, the eighty-year-old Mum of the pastor. The roving microphone person went over and Harry starts: "The most memorable Christmas I had was Bondi beach, lots of women and bee..." The microphone suddenly developed a fault so the rest couldn't be heard and the roving microphone person moved swiftly on to someone else. Amazingly the microphone started functioning again. On the way home, Daddy mentioned Harry's memorable Christmas to Mummy. Maisie asked what Daddy meant by "Lothario"? Mummy and Daddy decided to leave that explanation for a later date and changed the subject.

Nana, Opa and Geoff arrived. Opa had decided to ignore all the ideas that Mummy had suggested for the children's presents and instead presented the children with small cookbooks; so, Riley received a book on Brunches; Olly, Breakfasts; Nell, Tapas and Maisie got Desserts. Mummy wasn't sure that these books were entirely pitched at their age given that they were four, six, eight and nine and that Olly struggles to wipe his own butt never mind cook up Eggs Benedict.

Nana, on the other hand, is the Queen of knock-off toys, lots of them, Nana arrived with sacks of presents in tow, being carried in by an obliging Geoff who she had met on her way down the driveway. Mummy clocked the noisy toys with no volume control that Nana has gifted and syphoned them off to the pile that will be toys that remain at Nana's for the children to play with when they are there.

Christmas dinner was consumed by everyone except Riley who said he didn't feel very hungry, Mummy found out he had already eaten all of his selection box during the course of the morning.

A post-Christmas lunch walk, time to talk, Lego and games. A good day. Isla's first Christmas... Daddy woke Mummy from her snooze on the sofa and told her to go to bed. Time for some rest.

Epilogue

December 31st, 2021 (just...)

I put my pen down. Nothing much more to write for the period that is the no-man's land between Christmas and New Year. What a year that was. I think about what prompted me to start writing things down.

It was as we were clearing getting ready for the builders to start, just when I thought that I was managing quite well, I got totally taken by surprise by the bag full of memories I found in the corner of the dining room, Mum's stuff that Dad had dropped round when he had begun clearing out her things; Kenyan coins from a childhood adventure to Africa on a ship, song sheets for songs we used to sing over and over when we were little in the car on long journeys trekking across Europe, full to bursting with bright tissue paper, coloured pipe cleaners, stencils, card, coloured felt... just encapsulating the fun that Mum was. Always ready to make up a game or a story, always ready to sit and help with a school project or let us just create out of whatever we could find amongst her craft stuff. Realising she did this with her young students too (she was a teacher). A veritable treasure trove for the grandkids... and then I realised my tears were mingled up with the colourful tissue paper, candles, birthday banners that decorated the kitchen when it was my birthday, Mum making sure you knew you were number one on her priority list that day... so many memories. It makes you think; treasure the moments; when you are exhausted and feel like you have nothing more to give, for those moments are fleeting, but the memories of those moments can last a lifetime and impact generations to come. I am so thankful for my Mum. I write to myself on this New Year's Eve; you may blip on this parenting journey, it has its highs, its lows, its laughter and its tears. It can be so easy to see how you are getting it wrong, all the things that you're not doing, or all the things that you are doing that you shouldn't be, so easy to focus on those things and miss the bits where you are getting it right. It doesn't have to be grand holidays and expensive toys, it can be the little moments, time and you... you being present. Not busyness, just you. You are enough for these little people who love you to the core. You are enough for Him who loves you to the core.

Parenting; bedlam and beauty, marvellousness and mayhem all rolled into one.

About the Author

Jess Hymus-Gant lives and works in North Wales. Following some time working in Spain and Mexico City, she moved back to Wales and has worked as a Service Manager for a social justice charity for the past twenty-four years. She is passionate about helping people discover their worth, which is very much fuelled by her faith.

Jess loves being a Mum and Step-Mum to her six sons and three daughters and is forever being surprised by a new curve-ball that her kids throw at her, just when she thinks she has it sussed.

Headspace for Jess is painting, going for a run along the beach or a walk up a hill with her dogs, reading, gardening and baking. She loves a good coffee and belly-laughing with friends.

She has been married for twenty years and lives with her husband, two sons, three daughters and the two family dogs and a cat. xx

About PublishU

PublishU is transforming the world of publishing.

PublishU has developed a new and unique approach to publishing books, offering a three-step guided journey to becoming a globally published author!

We enable hundreds of people a year to write their book within 100-days, publish their book in 100-days and launch their book over 100-days to impact tens of thousands of people worldwide.

The journey is transformative, one author said,

"I never thought I would be able to write a book, let alone in 100 days... now I'm asking myself what else have I told myself that can't be done that actually can?'"

To find out more visit
www.PublishU.com

MOMENTS IN MUMMYDOM

Printed in Great Britain
by Amazon